W9-BMT-093

LIVING WITHOUT GOD

Living

WITHOUT

God

New Directions for Atheists, Agnostics,

Secularists, and the Undecided

Ronald Aronson

COUNTERPOINT

BERKELEY

Library of Congress Cataloging-in-Publication Data
Aronson, Ronald, 1938–
Living without God : new directions for atheists, agnostics,
secularists, and the undecided / Ronald Aronson.
p. cm.
1. Rationalism. 2. Atheism. 3. Atheism—United States.
4. Conduct of life. I. Title.
BL2747.A76 2008   211′.6—dc22
2008012035
1-59376-160-0
978-1-59376-160-8

Cover design by David Bullen
Interior design by David Bullen
Printed in the United States of America

COUNTERPOINT
2117 Fourth Street
Suite D
Berkeley, CA 94710
www.counterpointpress.com

Distributed by Publishers Group West

10 9 8 7 6 5 4 3 2 1

To the memory
of my grandfather and father,
Abraham Aronson and Saul Aronson,
and to my grandchildren,
Hannah Aronson-Paxton
and Zachary Aronson-Paxton

Contents

Acknowledgments

Inasmuch as gratitude is one of the main themes of this book, these pages have special meaning for me. The idea for *Living Without God* first occurred to me while I was a visiting professor at DePaul University in Chicago. Since then many people have cheered me on, given me ideas, sent me materials, and critically and appreciatively read some or all of this book—and without them it would not have been possible. I want to thank Jerry Deneau, Julie Klein, Caroline Maun, Marsha Richmond, Roslyn Schindler, Antonetta Johnson-Gardner, Carole Keller, Adrien van den Hoven, Ernst Benjamin, Miriam Jerris, Greg Epstein, Pamela Aronson, Nina Aronson, Marilyn Aronson, Barb House, Matt Eshleman, Ken Waltzer, Jonathan Judaken, Barbara Ching, David Brent, Raphael de Kadt, Rosalie Gold, Sam Rosenthall, and Doug Ireland. It has been a great pleasure to work with everyone at Counterpoint on the project, especially Jack Shoemaker, Trish Hoard, and Laura Mazer.

Portions of this book have appeared in *The Common Review*, *Bookforum*, *The Philosophers' Magazine*, *The Toronto Star*, *The Nation*, and the journal of the society for Humanistic Judaism. I have also presented my ideas to the Humanities Center, University of Memphis; the Philosophy Department, University of Toledo; the Camus and History Conference, University of Florida;

North American Sartre Society; the Philosophy Department, University of Windsor; the Adult Learning Institute at Oakland Community College; the Society of Active Retirees; and the Humanities Center, Wayne State University; as well as to my students in the Interdisciplinary Studies Program. During a sabbatical leave I was fortunate to be able to spend time as a fellow at the Wayne State University Humanities Center, directed by Walter Edwards.

In the summer of 2007 I worked on this book while in treatment for prostate cancer at the Weisberg Cancer Center of the Barbara Ann Karmanos Cancer Institute. It was an appropriate time to write chapter six, "Dying Without God." I want to thank everyone on the caring staff at Weisberg, and especially the radiation therapists who listened to and commented on my latest thoughts about death and dying.

I am especially grateful to those who have been closest to this project from beginning to end, helping me to find my voice, give this book its shape, and see it through to conclusion: Phyllis Aronson, Geri Thoma, Robert Deneweth, Danny Postel, Ira Konigsberg, Walter Poznanski, Mark Shapiro, and Steve Golin.

Living

WITHOUT

God

Turning Toward Something

WHETHER THEY CALL THEMSELVES ATHEISTS AND AFFIRM that God does not exist, or agnostics, disbelieving but less certain, or skeptics, humanists, unbelievers, or freethinkers, the number of Americans who find "meaning and value in life without looking to a god" is so great that they would constitute the majority of adults in all but a handful of countries in the world. Yet for most of the past generation in the United States, secularists, to use a term embracing all of the above, have lived under the spell cast by resurgent, aggressive, fundamentalist-tinged religion. They have grown used to opening their morning newspaper and seeing, as in the *New York Times* in February 2007, a large photograph of the Indianapolis Colts football team holding hands, heads bowed in prayer, thanking God for victory in the Super Bowl. Or seeing front-page articles in local newspapers such as the *St. Petersburg Times*, in February 2008, trumpeting the results of a statewide poll showing half of Floridians preferring the teaching of faith-based alternatives to evolution in public schools.

Or hearing the President calling us to prayer after a gunman's murder/suicide rampage, or when sending soldiers off to war. Or watching Democratic candidates testify to being guided by "the hand of God," as if they regarded being religious as essential a qualification for a president as having a strong position on national health insurance.

Secularists remember well that one of the most dramatic presidential addresses in American history, at the National Cathedral three days after September 11, 2001, was so filled with religious language that it was virtually a sermon. It was delivered by a president flanked by Jewish, Muslim, and Christian representatives, with no one invited to stand alongside them whose presence might acknowledge the existence of the tens of millions of secular Americans. At this most important collective moment in the recent history of the United States, it was as if they did not exist. The United States had become a nation of believers.

For a generation, secularists have been a timid minority, voiceless, on the defensive, routinely derided, both warned against and ignored at the same time. Five courageous authors have done much to break this spell. What began with publisher W. W. Norton taking a chance at the worst of times on a gutsy, hyperbolic, and idiosyncratic attack on religion by a graduate student in neuroscience, Sam Harris's *End of Faith*, has now grown into a remarkable intellectual wave. No less than five book titles soon joined this one on various best-seller lists—Daniel Dennett's *Breaking the Spell*, Richard Dawkins's *God Delusion*, Harris's *Letter to Christian America*, Victor Stenger's *God: The Failed Hypothesis*, followed by Christopher Hitchens's *God Is Not Great*.

Helped by the sense of scandal that surrounds the public discussion of atheism in America, Harris, Dawkins, Dennett, and Hitchens have become the kind of media stars who prompt automatic nods of recognition when an attack on them or television appearance by them is mentioned. They have broken a taboo in twenty-first-century America: Do not speak ill of religion. Suddenly responses, debates, interviews, and articles began appearing at every turn, and even medium-sized bookstores offered a dozen titles in newly created "atheism" sections, whose topics, in addition to the "new atheist" books, range from anthologies to secular child-rearing to zinger quotations.

The enormous wave of public interest owes itself first to the books themselves, blunt, no-holds-barred attacks on religion in different registers that are deliberately addressed to mainstream readers. Harris excoriates religious moderates as providing cover for fundamentalists at home and abroad by refusing to contest—because they share—the extremists' premises. More upbeat, Dennett is devoted to creating the intellectual conditions for future discussions, in which religion will be treated as just another "natural" phenomenon and accordingly subjected to critical scrutiny. The inexhaustible Dawkins bulldozes his way through every major argument and a great many minor ones for religious belief. And Hitchens wittily and relentlessly catalogues religion's crimes and absurdities. But why did they strike a chord in their readers that continues to reverberate among us? Pounding away with urgency and sledgehammer strength, they have collectively forced American secularists to realize how fed up they are with having become a quiet, apologetic, invisible minority.

A couple of generations ago, too, secularists were confident and on the offensive. In the 1920s and 1930s, those turning out to hear Clarence Darrow, a major national public figure on the lecture circuit, might crowd into a packed house to watch him simultaneously debate a rabbi, a priest, and a minister. The man *Variety* called America's greatest one-man attraction could stand before an audience and proudly say: "I don't believe in God because I don't believe in Mother Goose." By the 1960s it was common for educated people to assume that traditional religion was in steep decline. It was known that an increasing percentage of leading American scientists disbelieved or doubted the existence of God. Anyone who had taken introductory sociology was likely to have heard of Durkheim's "secularization" theory, according to which a decline in religious belief went hand in hand with modernization.

And most striking, the very idea of God was becoming confused and uncertain. As the personal and wonder-working Judeo-Christian God grew less and less plausible to modern and sophisticated people, it was more plausible to see religion undermined by urbanization, science, higher education, and the individualism and materialism of consumer society, losing its energy and becoming an irrelevant social phenomenon. The increasingly secularized modern world was witnessing an "apparent eclipse of God" among theologians, who were groping without agreement toward a contemporary image of a kind of "anonymous God." Accordingly, in April 1966, *Time* proclaimed that the very idea of God had become surrounded by doubt and confusion, asking, on a stark black pictureless cover and in red letters: "Is God Dead?" Its exploration of the long- and short-term trends making up the contemporary "problem of God" caused a sensation, perhaps because the cover seemed to be claiming much more than the article itself.

Not long after, John Lennon's "Imagine" reached the top of the sales charts by expressing a utopian vision of a world without war, greed, or hunger. Played endlessly over the past generation, it has become a familiar part of our mental furniture. According to the song, what exactly are the conditions for a society of peace, brotherhood, and sisterhood? Just before calling for doing away with possessions and living a life of sharing, the song expresses two wishes—that there be no countries to kill for or die for, and that there be no religion. It is a vision of a world without heaven or hell, with nothing above us but the sky: "Imagine all the people living for today . . . "

How times have changed. In 2005, *Bookforum* commemorated the *Time* cover story with its own cover article, by this author, asking, in the haunting red letters on black background, "Is God *Still* Dead?" My essay, about the new atheists, explored the weakened state of secularism in the United States in the context of the remarkable recent flourishing of religion.

This is the America where presidential invocations of God have increased enormously since the election of Ronald Reagan. While few loud-and-clear voices have been agitating in the mainstream on behalf of the separation of church and state, for secular and public education, or demanding less rather than more political discussion of religion, candidates outdo each other to demonstrate their religious credentials. In winter 2006 on the floor of the Senate, presidential candidate Hillary Clinton spoke against the bill that would have illegalized aid to undocumented immigrants by claiming that it violated her sense of the Bible and "would literally criminalize the Good Samaritan and probably even Jesus himself." That summer Barack Obama avowed his religious credentials for the presidential campaign, insisting that "secularists are wrong when they ask believers to leave their religion at the door before entering the public square." During the primary campaign it became increasingly common to hear Clinton's and Obama's religious beliefs.

The most striking example of candidates succumbing to the new religious correctness was Mormon Republican presidential candidate Mitt Romney's unintentional parody of John F. Kennedy's 1960 speech on religious tolerance and secularism. Kennedy had presented a dignified and thoughtful statement

on tolerance and secularism, simultaneously affirming his independence from Rome as a Catholic public official, the American
tradition of religious toleration, and his belief in "an America
where the separation of church and state is absolute." Romney
too spoke of toleration, but he simultaneously sought to reas-
sure conservative Christians that he was one of them and make
clear that his vision of America as a religion-based society had
no room for those wrongheaded people "intent on establishing
a new religion in America—the religion of secularism." This is
the America where in early 2007 an Arkansas bill to create a
Thomas Paine Day failed to pass the state house after a Republican representative "took exception to Paine's stated preference
for reason rather than religion." In our time, religion has become
so dominant a presence in American life that until Harris's *End
of Faith* appeared, the only people who dared to criticize it publicly were comics—Bill Maher on his own show and the Com-
edy Channel's Stephen Colbert and Robb Corddry on *The Daily
Show*'s "This Week in God."

Since its days of decline, and especially in the past twenty
years, as sociologist Alan Wolfe has shown with sensitivity and
appreciation, religion has revived itself remarkably, becoming a
thoroughly contemporary energizing force for tens of millions
of Americans. Roughly as many Americans accept the Bible's
creation story as they do evolution. In the George W. Bush White
House it became commonplace to begin meetings with prayers,
for people to say, reverentially, that they have been "chosen" for
their life path or that everything is "meant to happen," both presumably by God. We hear the same on talk shows, from athletes
being interviewed, and from fellow workers, friends, and family. CNN deemed it appropriate, in a Republican presidential

debate, to have a man hold up a Bible and ask the candidates: "Do you believe every word in this book?"

Not only has religion mounted a remarkable comeback in the United States, not only are Darrow's and Lennon's irreligious perspectives no longer taken for granted in the mainstream—today, the public display of belief in God has become the default assumption of American society. The once-standard formula for reconciling religion and politics by separating them into "private" and "public" spheres no longer works as the common sense of America. And this is not only the opinion of conservatives like Supreme Court justice Antonin Scalia: witness Obama's criticism of secularists and his assertive avowal of his religion in the public square. Despite repeated defeats in the courts, efforts are continuing to permit teaching creationism—now recast as "intelligent design"—in public school biology classes. The barrier between church and state has been growing more porous, and church-driven campaigns have narrowed abortion rights and confirmed discrimination against homosexuals as public policy. Once-otherworldly conservative denominations are now quite comfortable being aggressively public and political.

We all know the story of how the Republican party has harnessed this energy, placing evangelical Christians at the core of its coalition and embracing many religious demands—opposing stem-cell research, gay marriage, abortion rights, championing government aid to religious schools and faith-based social programs—and appointing judges sympathetic to all of these. So successfully have they framed the issues that, according to the Pew Research Center's 2006 report on religion and politics, fully 69% of Americans believe the canard that liberals have "gone too far in trying to keep religion out of schools and government."

Given our secular Constitution and its history, this absurdly mistaken view could only have emerged from an aggressive campaign of distortion. But it is in turn based on another distortion, the one that makes "nearly all" Americans religious. We have all heard the polls telling us that *virtually everyone* in America—indeed, well over 90% of the population—is "really" religious. But how does that square with the thirty million adults who describe themselves as being without religion (14%–16% of adult Americans)? Or the one in six Americans who say that religion is "not too important" or "not at all important" in their lives? Or the one in every four Americans who declare themselves as "spiritual but not religious"? Or the one in four who are atheists, agnostics or "would prefer not to say"? These are among the disparate results of several different surveys asking different questions and interested in different issues. The remarkable diversity of results is bewildering until we realize that what the various surveys are committed to studying is what they measure best—just as the most "newsworthy" results are those indicating that almost all Americans are religious because the press has decided this is what is most interesting.

A secularist will look at the surveys rather differently than someone determined to confirm how religious Americans are. The Baylor Religion Survey (*American Piety in the 21st Century*), which bills itself as "the most extensive and sensitive study of religion ever conducted," triumphantly adjusted the thirty million people who have no religion *downward* to exclude those who do not belong to a religion but still believe in a God. Yet this survey strains the facts of belief by including all those who marked boxes preceding the following statements (their emphasis): "I have *no doubts* that God exists," "I believe in God, but with *some doubts*," "*I sometimes believe* in God," *and* "I believe in a *higher power or cosmic force*." In other words, Baylor counts *as religious* people who consider themselves not religious but "spiritual," casting a vast net over adherents of everything from history to cosmic energy to love. Then they allow only a single alternative: "I *don't believe* in anything beyond the physical world." In short, they overcount believers and simply don't count many of those who regard themselves as agnostics or skeptics, secularists or humanists.

The 2008 Pew U.S. Religious Landscape Survey is the most sophisticated and detailed study of religious identification. It tallies over 16% of the people as atheists, agnostics, and those whose religion is "nothing in particular." Like Baylor, it shows that a sizable percentage of these—Pew reports 6%—are religious even though unaffiliated. But interestingly enough, it also asks people how important religion is in their lives: very important, somewhat important, not too important, or not at all important? Its results: 56%, 26%, 9%, and 7%, respectively. Perhaps more important than these statistics is the fact that the Baylor and Pew surveys, in both their framing and their reporting, were studying above all the shades of belief and belonging, and accordingly treated religion and denominational identification with a sense of nuance and complexity denied to the various shades of disbelief. And neither remarked on the "social desirability effect"—poll respondents may be reluctant to give an unpopular answer, such as appearing insufficiently religious.

This may help explain the strikingly different result of the *Newsweek*/Beliefnet survey measuring the importance of spirituality. Respondents were asked to identify themselves as either "spiritual but not religious," "religious but not spiritual," "religious and spiritual, "not spiritual/not religious," or "don't know." The totals in these categories were 24%, 9%, 55%, 8%, and 4%, respectively. That is, nearly one in four respondents chose "spiritual but not religious" when given a socially desirable way of declaring themselves as not being religious. The total that chose *not* to identify as religious in this survey is a remarkable 36%. Clearly, depending on how the questions are asked and the purposes of the study, spirituality, like secularism, can be made to virtually disappear—or to appear—as a major trend of contemporary American life.

What would we find if unbelief was given as much attention as belief? The *Financial Times*/Harris Interactive survey of Europeans and Americans allowed respondents the opportunity to identify themselves as follows: "Believer in any form of God or any type of supreme being," "Agnostic (one who is skeptical about the existence of God but not an atheist)," "Atheist (one who denies the existence of God)," "Would prefer not to say," and "Not sure." The results? 4% of Americans are atheists, 14% are agnostics, 6% choose not to answer, and 3% are not sure—an arguably secularist response of one in four.

At least two identifiable streams of the "not very religious" increase the numbers of the secular-minded. First are church members for whom religion is either unimportant or not very important. The Pew survey reports the total, including the irreligious, as one in six Americans. We might include among these all those who nominally belong to a religion but are actually unbelievers; who describe themselves as members of a religion but effectively live without any active relationship either to it or to God; who belong to a church and attend services but are "tacit atheists" living day in and day out with only token reference to God; and those who are "too damn busy" to think about God.

Second, I would include many of those identified in the most significant finding of the Baylor survey—namely, that over one in four American believers in God do not mean a personal God at all but a "distant God" that "is not active in the world and not especially angry either." According to the study, "These individuals tend toward thinking of God as a cosmic force which set the laws of nature in motion. As such, God does not 'do' things in the world and does not hold clear opinions about our activities or world events." Of the four Gods believed in by Americans, this one sounds like the cosmic force or energy spoken of by spiritualists, or the deist God of "unbelievers" Thomas Jefferson and Thomas Paine. It would seem that believers in this God certainly live quite secular lives.

There are tens of millions of Americans who are irreligious or "not very religious" or "spiritual." They believe in no God or in something bearing little resemblance to the traditional Jewish, Christian, or Muslim Gods; or whatever their belief or belonging, they live mostly secular lives. In addition, there are tens of millions of secular-minded believers. Many of these belong to the liberal religions, Jewish and Christian (especially those denominations belonging to the National Council of Churches such as the United Church of Christ and the Episcopal and Presbyterian churches), and have long practice in accommodating themselves to science and the modern world and embrace the separation of church and state. Among these are believers who remain inspired by Genesis but refuse to take it in "literal, factual terms."

All told, this vast number of secularists and the secular-minded may help to explain, as the Pew Religion & Politics survey tells us, that depending on the survey question, 15% to 49% of Americans are either secular on issues of church and state, religious but scientific-minded, or troubled by the current expansion of religion in American life. The Pew survey reports only 17% of Americans wanting to see less religious influence on American life but fully 32% wanting less religious influence on government. In 2006, 28% said that President Bush talked too much about his religious faith and prayer, and the same number denied that the U.S. was a Christian nation. Most dramatically, a whopping 49% believed that Christian conservatives had "gone too far in trying to impose their religious values on the country."

These, then, are the two great unnoticed and unreported secrets of American life: first, a sizable minority live their lives without a traditionally or organizationally defined God or religion; and second, considerable numbers of religious and secular Americans have been becoming fed up with the in-your-face religion that has come to mark our society. Now it is customary to read many of these results from the opposite direction in order to show just how overwhelmingly Americans embrace the Bible and religion in government and just how underwhelmingly they accept evolution. But what I am asking about is, after all, an enormous minority on the other side. My point is that the constant media drumbeat emphasizing the huge percentages embracing religion has paid little attention to those people, religious, secular, or in between, who find themselves unhappy with the current piety and who themselves are an important minority deserving no less consideration than other minorities, especially in light of our secular Constitution.

Despite their current political invisibility, both unbelievers and secular-minded believers sense themselves as a beleaguered but coherent and essential part of American society, facing an antiscientific and anti-intellectual trend in a country in which conservative Christianity and politicians have recently dominated public space.

Ironically, the most widespread mainstream political response to the power of evangelical Christians has been to call for *more* religion in politics, not less, but this time from the left. Mainstream Democratic politicians have been making much of their faith, and a religious left has been taking shape to counteract the conservative Christian complicity with war and environmental destruction. Meanwhile, few loud and clear voices have been agitating in the mainstream on behalf of the separation of church and state, for secular and public education, or to demand less, not more, public discussion of religion.

The aggressive nature of the religious revival, including over-zealous polling, is one reason why those of us who live without God have allowed ourselves to be pushed to the margins of pub-lic discourse. But it is not the only one. That secularists have lost confidence over the past generation also reveals some particular weakness among us, either in our own outlook, self-image, or relationship to our historical world. This world no longer seems to be going our way, but also our way no longer seems as clearly marked as it once was. Atheists, agnostics, and secularists have traditionally blamed religion for many of the world's woes, and it would not be surprising to do the same in explaining our own. But it is a bad habit. It avoids looking inward and confronting the secular loss of vision.

According to professor of theology and Anglican priest Alister McGrath, those who live without God are on the defen-sive because their outlook has grown old, stopped adapting to the world, and thus lost its relevance. In his celebratory formu-lation, we are living in the "twilight" of the great modern era of disbelief. By proclaiming that atheism is on its last legs, McGrath turns one of the most burning questions in American culture on its head. When everyone is asking about the growing strength of religion and its political ramifications, he instead asks: Why is disbelief on the wane? His postmodern answer is that "the reli-gion of the autonomous and rational human being, who believes that reason is able to uncover and express the deepest truths of the universe, from the mechanics of the rising of the sun to the nature and final destiny of humanity," has become less and less relevant to people's needs today. At his own personal turning point, he discovered that his own atheism and Marxism were an "imaginatively impoverished and emotionally deficient substitute for a dimension of life that I had hitherto suppressed." As he converted to religion and joined history's next wave, the works of atheism's golden age lost their aura of historical inevitability, now seeming distant, redolent of "a social order that had long since vanished." This is why atheism is now adrift in a newly respiritualized world, a curiosity "uncertain of its own values."

And McGrath suggests, although he does not recount it, that there is a story behind the secularist timidity and uncertainty today, one that dates back to the very origins of the Enlightenment assault on religion. I tell this story in chapter one, and will inventory the baggage of secularism, especially its essential link to the idea of Progress, which promised so much and came to such grief during the twentieth century. What is called for today, if a twenty-first-century revival of secularism is to be possible, is to free it from its original historical premises and false hopes. To live comfortably without God today means doing what has not yet been done—namely, rethinking the secular worldview after the eclipse of modern optimism. This can happen only by working through the secular outlook itself, in light of the disasters and disappointments of the last century, and dangers of this one.

To appreciate our problem, atheists, agnostics, and skeptics need only recall the hesitations and stammerings of their most recent personal conversations with anyone who is religious. Even after reading Harris, Dennett, Dawkins, or Hitchens, secularists have difficulty discussing what it is we believe in, if not God. Our own point of view, once so robust and filled with energy, is diffident and measured, able to respond to religious enthusiasm only with our denial of God followed by our own uncertainties. In contrast to our principled tentativeness, our religious friends affirm their belief in the coherence of the universe and the world, their deep sense of belonging to it and to a human community, their refusal to be stymied by the limits of their knowledge, their confidence in dealing with life's mysteries and uncertainties, their willingness to take complete responsibility for the small things while leaving forces beyond themselves in charge of the large ones, their security in knowing right from wrong, and perhaps above all, their sense of hope about the future. Even if we would reject these beliefs as unfounded and irrational, we have to be struck by their force. And envy their coherence. In response, what do we have to say about the latest research into religion's effectiveness, for example, in helping people withstand and bounce back from illness and disease? Why are we unable to be more persuasive? Besides disbelief, what do we have to offer? What should we tell our children and grandchildren as we see them swept up in a pervasively religious environment?

These questions begin where Harris's *End of Faith* and the other books leave off. Harris may exude intellectual clarity in relation to those who live by faith rather than evidence, and Dawkins speaks loudly for science and rationality against irrationality and self-delusion. Their goal is to combat religion with hard-edged and rational demand for evidence, not to explore the weaknesses and needs of their own point of view. In attacking religion the authors have been breaking the prohibition against talking about it seriously, and they may certainly be forgiven for not being calmer or more measured. Doing battle with what they see as the most pervasive and bothersome phenomenon in American life during the past generation, Harris, Dennett, Dawkins, and Hitchens deserve praise for their courage and tenacity in shattering its spell. They belong to the time-honored tradition of frontal attack by atheists on religion. But although drawing energy from them, this is not what I am doing in this book.

Nor am I following the second customary approach: the strategy of *explaining* religion. Starting with Lucretius's statement that religion is rooted in fear of the unknown, this line of thought came to its own in the nineteenth century in the writings of Feuerbach, Marx, and Freud, and has been brought up to date in Dennett's *Breaking the Spell.* These writers begin from the premise that religion is a false belief, but that it originates in a genuine human need. Due to our capacity for enlightenment, or because of new historical possibilities, or as a result of our understanding of human evolution, we are now able to free ourselves from religion.

Unlike either group of writings, this book offers the reader little criticism or examination of religion. I address myself to those who know that our labor is not yet done when we have broken its spell, or who are weary of continuing the argument against religion as if it were the enemy. Religion is not really the issue, but rather the incompleteness or tentativeness, the thinness or emptiness, of today's atheism, agnosticism, and secularism. Living without God means turning toward something. To flourish we need coherent secular popular philosophies that effectively answer life's vital questions.

When I first published this thought, in the *Nation* in summer 2007, it provoked considerable criticism from fellow secularists. "What we don't need," said one of them, "is another elaborate construct that pretends to answer life's questions." Another said, "I don't want any substitute for religion. I hold myself responsible for ethics, morality, or whatever makes a responsible person." As the reader will see, I agree that it would be a mistake to replace institutionalized religion with such substitutes as the various forms of belief in Progress. But, as I will also argue in this book, it is no less of a mistake to replace it with the belief that life's important questions cannot be answered or with a reflexive prejudice for individualistic ethics and against seeing ourselves socially. We are not part of a dominant wave of human betterment that is ineluctably transforming the world, nor are we adrift and alone in an absurd universe. But, as I will argue in constructing a secular guide to reflection and action, we are deeply embedded in nature, history, and society in ways that give our lives meaning and impose demands on us.

My starting point is that one-quarter of a millennium after the beginning of the Enlightenment, it is still so very, very hard to be human. Death, loss, suffering, and inhumanity form an essential frame within which our lives take place. And, after so much civilization, we live in a dizzying universe of "despites"—despite all that humans have done to transform nature into a habitable environment, we are ruining the environment; despite dazzling accomplishments in medicine and public health, most humans are insecure about having adequate healthcare; despite a global economy that places the rest of the world in our own lives, our ancestors' dependence on nature has been replaced by our own economic vulnerability; despite generations of struggles for dignity and equality, the global distribution of wealth and power are fundamentally unequal and unfair. And so on, endlessly, multiplying paradoxes until the insecurities and miseries of most lives rival those of the past.

In such a world is it any wonder that people turn to religion? It consoles and offers hope. It provides answers to some of life's most perplexing problems. It gives meaning and promises justice. Its roots lie not only in the deep past, our ignorance, or even in our refusal to live without myth. Religion's roots also lie in the stresses of our experience. Young Karl Marx called religion the "heart of a heartless world," and we might also think of it as the meaning of a meaningless world, and the order of an absurd world. It is hardly a surprising response to this life and this world, which remain hard and inhospitable.

So living without God means not simply rejecting God, but asking and answering vital existential questions still at the heart of today's religions. These were once persuasively addressed by secularists, but they have reemerged to taunt the twenty-first century with new urgency. Why is life so harsh? Where does human destructiveness come from? Why does our organized and rationalized world seem so irrational? Why, despite movement after movement on behalf of justice, is life still so unfair? Is there reason to hope that any of this can be improved? What is the meaning and direction of human life, without God and after Progress? What are our prospects for understanding the world today? How can we act morally? How can we come to terms with the specter of our own death? These are questions about how to think, how to see ourselves, and how to live in this century. My answers will be presented in chapters two through seven, and will form a kind of twenty-first-century guide for the perplexed.

As a secularist, I intend to answer the questions in terms of this world and this life, without resorting to quasi-religious terms like "soul," "transcendent," "spirit," and "spiritual." Usually used in vague and imprecise ways, such terms often point toward layers of experience that call for more explanation. I hope that this book will locate many of these as concrete and understandable experiences of our lives. Most of us are so rooted in religious traditions that we have difficulty finding precise and secular language to describe them. Yet, with some effort, we have all the tools we need to make sense of our lives. But it should be obvious that many people, whether religious or not, live parts of their lives at extreme variance with other parts, have beliefs that contradict their actions, express sentiments on a given day that are inconsistent with how they live the rest of the week, and hold dear to some ideas that go sharply against other of their beliefs. Consistency is a great virtue, and so my answers to these questions will aim for, and deserve to be judged by how well they achieve, a coherence absent from much current religious and secular thinking today.

What sort of book is this, then? The first chapter explores the shipwreck of the worldview that secularism originally contained. In the rest I have sought to develop several original directions, including discussions of gratitude and dependence, aging and dying, responsibility and hope. I rely on classical writings as well as outstanding recent specialized work by philosophers, political scientists, sociologists, evolutionary biologists, historians, physicians, and educators . My purpose is to begin a conversation with the wider community that is nontechnical and experience-oriented. Accordingly, this book belongs to the tradition in philosophy and the history of ideas that reaches back to Socrates and Plato and continues through the Enlightenment, Marx, Nietzsche, Camus, Sartre, and my teacher Herbert Marcuse.

But it is also something more. When hearing me lecture in South Africa as the struggle against apartheid was coming to a climax, in 1987, one of my hosts, educated at Oxford, called me a "secular preacher" with an ironic smile on his face. Certainly he was paying tribute to what he perceived as my passion and commitment (by my next visit, in 1990, he had left South Africa to teach in Britain), but he also was needling me for my departure from his standards of academic balance and objectivity. "Secular" of course contains its own reply, namely that however impassioned, whatever I say is to be rationally evaluated and judged by the available evidence.

I assume that my readers will not be primarily experts and

will belong to the huge stream of unaffiliated secularists, secular humanists, skeptics, freethinkers, agnostics, and atheists—and even "spiritualists"—who are trying to find their way through today's life issues and negotiate today's world on their own, without religion. And they may also include religious people who are questioning their own direction.

I also hope that my ideas spark discussion among the small but vital current of organized secular humanists that has been attempting to answer many of the questions I discuss, holding conferences, publishing magazines, and taking positions on important issues. They have sometimes produced alternative forms of religion, complete with ministers, sanctuaries, and services. They have, however, not been able to kindle much fire beyond the narrow group of those who already identify as secular humanists or belong to one of their organizations. But they have made a major contribution by acting on the understanding that living without God requires a labor of construction. They deserve praise for thinking through what it means to be secular and daring to create nonreligious rituals and life paths. Just as I admire but am critical of their work, I hope they will enter into spirited conversation with my ideas.

I also address myself to those in more secularized societies outside of the United States, especially in Europe and Japan, who may be puzzled by the remarkable contemporary paradox that the quintessential American believers in modernity—atheists, agnostics, and secularists—have been virtually voiceless in the society whose modern ways of life have become the worldwide norm, whose people are far more individualistic than Europeans, and whose educational institutions have long been regarded as setting the world's standard. Why should secularism here be weak while it has been gaining force in similar societies and cultures elsewhere, and although the United States has far milder reasons for disillusionment with the modern world? Why is it that in Western Europe, after two wars, totalitarian dictatorships, and genocide, secularism continues to advance even as Enlightenment optimism peters out?

Former archbishop of Canterbury George Carey once drew attention to the prevalence of "tacit atheism" in Britain as total Anglican Sunday church attendance in the UK dipped below one million (only 4% of nominal church members). Western Europeans live increasingly without God, and one-third fewer Canadians claim to attend church regularly than Americans. But although these societies are diverging from the United States, explicit atheism is not exactly flourishing anywhere, and people in other advanced societies seem comfortable leading secular lives while remaining nominal church members. One gets the sense that little effort is being devoted to reconciling lives that are becoming increasingly irreligious with the institutions and belief systems people have inherited. But sooner or later they will face the need to develop worldviews that are coherent and consistent with their lives. Although my specific references are often American, I think the deeper issues are common to all of us.

I seek to provide food for thought to all these readers. I know well that I am presenting only one of many possible secular worldviews. I welcome the fact that others will dispute my list of essential questions, and will argue for better answers than the ones I give. For example, my most original discussions are about gratitude, responsibility, dying, and hope. Am I right to argue that these are the central issues? I seek to encourage and provoke discussion about such questions, and to add my voice to what I expect to become a major new current.

After Progress

TIME WAS WHEN ANYONE LIKELY TO OPEN A BOOK WITH a title like *Living Without God* would have shared certain assumptions with the author (and other readers). Disbelief in God was only one of these. All would certainly have believed in Progress, the shared conviction that human life had improved over time and was continuing to improve. Its causes might be science and technology, the spread and deepening of education, economic growth, or social and political developments such as democracy or socialism. All these forms of betterment were going hand in hand with human enlightenment. Most readers would probably have equated Progress with that other hope that has virtually vanished today, voiced confidently at the beginning of the Enlightenment by Frederick the Great: "The human soul has shaken off the yoke of superstition and gained the courage to use its reason." This sentiment was taken up and amplified by speakers and writers over the next two centuries, and the main superstition from which people were freeing themselves was religion.

By the last quarter of the nineteenth century these optimistic voices were a dominant European and American chorus influencing educated and popular thinking. Ludwig Feuerbach, Karl Marx, and Charles Darwin each contributed to the current that received its most startling expression in Nietzsche's statement "God is dead," published in 1882. At about the same time, Robert Ingersoll, America's great agnostic whose traces have been all but obliterated, was giving voice to such thoughts in less outrageous but more directly public ways, to audiences around the United States. As Susan Jacoby says in *Freethinkers*, this was our "Golden Age of freethought," and as its leading figure Ingersoll knit together enlightenment, progress, and irreligion in singing popular prose:

> Forward, oh sublime army of progress, forward until law is justice, forward until ignorance is unknown, forward while there is a spiritual or temporal throne, forward until superstition is a forgotten dream, forward until the world is free, forward until human reason, clothed in the purple of authority, is king of kings.

In this his first public lecture, "Progress," and throughout his life, Ingersoll identified the major obstacles to advancement as religion and the "ghosts" it conjured up to oppress humans and stupefy their reason. His prescription for overcoming its power could have come straight from Feuerbach's *Essence of Christianity* a half century earlier: "The first step toward progress is for man to cease to be the slave of the creatures of his creation." For Ingersoll and his audience, living without such superstitions as God was a daring but nonetheless logical deduction from, and further contribution to, the enormous advances in science, democracy, and education occurring at every turn. He implored his listeners to banish the ghosts and rely on their own reason, inventiveness, and labor power. "All that gives us better bodies and minds and clothes and food and pictures, grander music, better heads, better hearts, and that makes us better husbands and wives and better citizens, all these things combined produce what we call the progress of the human race."

This is the kind of exuberant optimism, the sense of being connected to a great and soon-to-be-victorious historical trend, "the holy cause of human progress," that readers once would have brought to a book like this. But that was then. Today, for all our advances in education and science, all our rational self-calculations and forms of social organization, who is so optimistic anymore? The "Golden Age" is long over, not even a memory. And more recently, we have quietly bade goodbye to what Ingersoll called "the angel of Progress." After Progress, what is the situation of atheists, agnostics, and secularists in the first decade of the twenty-first century?

Today's reader wanting to reflect on living without God is probably, like everyone else, troubled about where the world is heading. She is not so likely to see secular living as the next exhilarating personal step in a world marked by other hopeful trends. Chances are that she is looking for bearings, just hoping to get along as a secularist in religious America. Unlikely anymore to see herself as part of a vanguard, she may experience herself as beleaguered and out of step with her surroundings.

If she lives outside a few major urban or university centers, in the vast heartland of suburban and semirural America, she has grown accustomed to new acquaintances greeting her by asking what church she goes to. At work, she'll have gotten used to God-talk as an unstated norm, having to decide again and again whether to "out" herself or to just remain silent. She'll wrestle with whether to be so mean-spirited as to challenge the well-meaning people who wish her a blessed day or, in times of crisis, make sure she's in their prayers. Reading newspapers or watching television, she'll also be used to hearing that the appropriate response to stressful situations is to turn to God, that the president, football and baseball teams, and headline writers all have prayer on their minds during wartime, before and after big games, and in response to disasters or murderous rampages. She'll also have grown accustomed to hearing offhand insults, news anchors reporting on combat sagely declaring that "there are no atheists in foxholes," would-be presidents criticizing secularists for trying to keep religion out of public places, would-be vice-presidents asserting that religion is necessary if one is to be a moral person. If she should go to the hospital, she'll be asked to state her religion, and once again will have to fake it or be bold enough to say "None," hoping that this raises no eyebrows.

In response to living out of the American mainstream, a non-believer may come to feel a bit defensive and self-protective rather than self-confident and path-breaking. She may be wondering about how to raise her children among other families who speak so often of church and God and prayer. She may even be unsure of what she believes, struggling to answer her own and others' questions, belonging to no circle, informal or formal, where she might explore her doubts and clarify her thinking. She is, in short, less likely to be looking outward to change the world and more likely searching for personal clarity, like-minded people, and even breathing space.

The she I'm talking about is a real, not a hypothetical, person. She shared her concerns with me after I gave a talk on the ideas in this book. In fact, she lives in the suburbs of a major American city, has two young children, and worries about how to raise them in God's country. Her situation represents an enormous turnabout from a hundred years ago. But is she really as outnumbered as it seems? As I indicated in the introduction, her

sense of isolation is exaggerated by a media and political disposition to fawn on religion and the religious. She is told constantly
that over 90% of Americans believe in God, and yet the actual
numbers are considerably less. And typically, when surveying the
unbelievers, the Baylor survey allowed atheists, agnostics, and
religious skeptics like my reader only a single choice, of agreeing
with the puzzling statement: "I don't believe in anything beyond
the physical world." Although in no way religious, I suspect that
she, like myself, would have a hard time checking a box that
appears to rule out commitments to values such as freedom and
justice, as well as emotions such as love.

The polls also hide the fact that almost all modern lives have
become overwhelmingly secular, meaning that, in both industrial
and postindustrial societies, government, the media, corpora-
tions, shopping, entertainment, sports and leisure, the healthcare industry, a vast array of counselors, experts and teachers,
and endless personal rational calculations have occupied most
of the ground that religion and religion-suffused activity used
to occupy. Modern life itself has consigned religion to a non-
rational inner space, except when shared with one's coreligion-
ists. Today, even intensely religious lives are mostly secular most
of the time.

In other words, it is possible to argue that even in countries
like the United States, despite my reader's trepidation, religion
is in deep trouble today. As sociologist Steve Bruce points out,
apparent signs of religious revitalization such as we see all around
us may on a deeper level amount to taking steps *away* from religion. Megachurch pastors must worry about the market- and
media-driven superficiality in some of today's religious revival.
For example, widely publicized surveys indicate that most evangelical youth are not staying in the fold as adults. "In every aspect
of the religious life, American faith has met American culture,"

sociologist Alan Wolfe tells us, "—and American culture has triumphed." When thinking about the individualistic, narcissistic, therapeutic, heavily marketed, doctrineless, and increasingly generic religion Wolfe describes, it is fair to ask with Bruce whether this isn't actually a stage of secularization en route to the fading of religion itself.

As the Baylor survey demonstrates, almost one in four Americans claim to believe in a God who has nothing to do with the world or themselves—a sort of deist God. And as I pointed out in the introduction, when survey questions leave space for genuine answers from those who regard themselves as agnostics, doubters, skeptics, secularists, or humanists, as well as those who "would prefer not to say," approximately one in four Americans do not believe in God or a supreme being. Biased, overzealous, or simply unthinking polling has been systematically inflating the numbers of American believers and hiding the number of secularists, over-reporting the first and under-reporting the second. If we were to add this nearly one-quarter to the nearly one-quarter of the Baylor respondents whose God is not involved with the world or ourselves, we might easily conclude that nearly half of all Americans reside in a vast uncharted and undiscussed land from which God is either absent or where he scarcely puts in an appearance. Suddenly the American believer/unbeliever relationship would be dramatically altered.

Moreover, if our reader ventures overseas, not only to Northern Europe but even to Italy or Spain, she will discover that she's far from being the tiny minority she seems to be in the United States. All these countries, as well as the other advanced societies, report far higher rates of disbelief than the United States; in England, France, or the Netherlands, for example, she would be joining the majority. Worldwide, she can in fact point to a not insignificant global number of the like-minded—those who regard themselves as atheists are conservatively estimated at between a half-billion and three quarters of a billion people worldwide.

Nevertheless, the United States is different. America is a Christian nation, say James Dobson, Pat Robertson, Chuck Colson, Tim and Beverly LaHaye, and Bill Gothard. While we have strongly diverged from the rest of the advanced world in the past generation, the Scopes trial should remind us that fundamentalism was already powerful early in the twentieth century, even at a time when atheism and agnosticism were in the air and vigorous. After that trial, educated Americans lulled themselves into thinking that fundamentalism had evaporated as a major force. After all, weren't those who H. L. Mencken called the "primates," "yokels," "morons," and "Neanderthals" of rural Tennessee humiliated before a national radio and newspaper audience?

Fifteen years later, in 1940, in a relatively unknown episode, the eminent British philosopher Bertrand Russell, widely known as an atheist and pacifist, was appointed to a short stint as a professor of philosophy at the City College of New York. Before he could begin teaching, a storm of protest centering on Russell's unconventional writings on sexual morality led to his appointment being rescinded by a judge's decision that he was "morally unfit to teach." Mayor Fiorello LaGuardia personally excised from the budget the amount earmarked for paying Russell, as democratically elected officials caved in under the pressure generated by church-sponsored organizations to keep the future recipient of the Nobel Prize for literature from lecturing on his first area of expertise, the philosophy of mathematics, at New York's renowned free public college. In a 1930 essay Russell himself had rhapsodized about humanity being on the threshold of "universal happiness," cautioning that "it will be necessary first to slay the dragon that guards the door, and this dragon is religion." But Russell himself could not get past the dragon-doorkeeper in the great modern city of New York.

Like the Scopes trial, this tempest turned out to be a harbinger of things to come. By century's end the most-discussed American social and political development was the revival of fundamentalist-tinged evangelical Christianity and its spread as a political force, soon to be ensconced in the White House. Presidents Carter, Reagan, and Clinton had prepared the way, either making much of their deep religious belief or using religion for political purposes, or both. By the George W. Bush presidency, religion's public flourishing was evidenced in countless ways, the most galling being efforts to pass new state and local laws restricting the teaching of evolution and promoting the teaching of Creationism, the most ludicrous being then–attorney general John Ashcroft's decision to cover the bare breast of the statue of "The Spirit of Justice" in his offices.

During this time, and wholly confuting the expectations of Robert Ingersoll, religious Americans have been refashioning their religions into institutions less driven by doctrine and authority, less judgmental, more concerned with the here and now. They have been modernizing their religion. Ingersoll and other nineteenth-century secularists would be most astounded by the fact that these religious Americans are doing so as a free people, no longer uneducated, not dominated by oppressive rulers or a rigid class system, not set upon by a government-supported clergy. They are geographically, socially, and economically mobile. As consumers in a market society, they are choosing religions increasingly that are more accepting and less fearsome, that are light on theology, and that blur the differences between denominations. By their choices they are remaking American religion.

Having survived the "God is dead" moment of the 1960s, religion has once again become a living force. This, as much as its newfound and democratic political power, was wholly unanticipated by the Enlightenment, the Golden Age of free thought, or by the sociological theories of secularization that had forecast religion's demise as societies became modern.

What explains this climate change? Why is the United States so religious today compared with other advanced societies? Obviously the exceptional phenomenon of American religiosity needs to be understood in relation to other countries. Some scholars who have done this reject the secularization theory, and have been seeking to replace it with the "supply-side" theory. This credits the absence of a state religion, and the resulting competition for adherents among a variety of churches, for higher rates of religious belief in the U.S. In other words, in a free market (as opposed to a state-supported monopoly), people are able to create religious institutions more responsive to their needs—and therefore religion flourishes.

With this argument in mind, social scientists Pippa Norris and Ronald Inglehart examined several societies characterized by great religious diversity and no state religion, and found little correlation with degrees of religiosity. They found that when societies are classified into the developmental categories of agrarian, industrial, and postindustrial, religious belief and practice do indeed decrease significantly from one stage to the next. The key to this decline turns out to be the extent to which "existential vulnerability is alleviated." People become less religious not when there are fewer religions to choose from—the "supply-side theory"—but when their lives are more secure. To say that religion provides a feeling of security in a dangerous and insecure world is to not speak subjectively or vaguely, but to point at very specific trends of human development—including how modern a society is, how secure its people are, and how equal they are. Using the World Values Survey, Norris and Inglehart make their case with impressive concreteness: that "a few basic developmental indicators such as per capita GNP, rates of AIDS/HIV, access to an improved water source, or the number of doctors per 100,000 people, predicted with remarkable precision how frequently the people of a given society worshiped or prayed." Vulnerability and insecurity, it turns out, drive religiosity.

It is a simple, powerful story: as a society moves into the later stages of industrialization, and as living conditions become less harsh and people live longer, they also become less religious. Yet how can this explain the United States, perennially one of the world's richest and yet most religious societies? Some of our puzzlement disappears when we look more closely. It was not the aggregate wealth of societies, but its wide distribution that began to protect masses of people against illness and poverty, as well as some of the worst traumas of old age. In highly developed societies this resulted from the emergence of the welfare state. And so the keys to secularization are: economic equality, education, literacy, income, healthcare, and social welfare. Two sets of facts thus help explain American religiosity today: Americans in general face higher levels of insecurity than inhabitants of other postindustrial societies, and American society is among the most unequal of all of them.

Norris and Inglehart deserve to be heard at length on these points, as they tell a familiar story, now connected with research that leads them to draw a striking conclusion:

> Relatively high levels of economic insecurity are experienced by many sectors of U.S. society, despite American affluence, due to the cultural emphasis on the values of personal responsibility, individual achievement, and mistrust of big government, limiting

the role of public services and the welfare state for basic matters such as healthcare covering all the working population. Many American families, even in the professional middle classes, face risks of unemployment, the dangers of sudden ill health without adequate private medical insurance, vulnerability to becoming a victim of crime, and the problems of paying for long-term care of the elderly. Americans face greater anxieties than citizens in other advanced industrialized countries about whether they will be covered by medical insurance, whether they will be fired arbitrarily, or whether they will be forced to choose between losing their job and devoting themselves to their newborn child. The entrepreneurial culture and the emphasis on personal responsibility has delivered overall prosperity but one trade-off is that the United States has greater income inequality than any other advanced industrial democracy.

As a result, Americans are more religious than are inhabitants of other wealthy societies. If people grow up where survival is insecure, they are more likely to be raised to be religious; if they grow up in conditions of security, religion will become less important to them. Indeed, Americans who are relatively well off are half as likely to be religious as those who are poor. There is a link between human progress and the growth of secularization, Norris and Inglehart conclude, but it moves in the opposite direction to the one originally proposed by secularization theory: it is not so much that modernization produces a decline in religious belief as that this happens during the later stages of modernization—insofar as human security increases.

Yet secularization is not produced automatically by improved living conditions, since it can be accelerated, retarded, or diverted by national, historical, cultural, and political factors, such as those operating in the United States. Understanding the United States fully also demands including core aspects of our national identity. One of these is the fact that this country took shape as a haven for many seeking religious freedom. This led simultaneously to a secular Constitution and to a rich and diverse religious landscape, which was part of our national character from the very beginning. Our history does matter, which means that the "supply-side theory" cannot be jettisoned so easily. Today, our greater religiosity and our greater existential vulnerability are both components of American national identity—each may by now be operating to strengthen the other.

Another core feature of American life from the beginning has been immigration to and movement around the continent, including unprecedented social as well as geographical mobility. This has contributed to another feature of our personality, America's strong individualism, which from the start may have fed, and today may still be feeding, the need for religious belonging. So yes, Americans are more religious, have less of a welfare state, have greater existential vulnerability, and are more individualistic—and each of these is probably encouraged by and buttresses the others.

Does this explanation, plus the recent aggressive politicization of religion, account for the predicament in which today's reader finds herself? Not completely. As I suggested in the introduction, today there is a problem with disbelief itself. One would not think so from the self-confident and aggressive stance of a Dennett, a Dawkins, or a Harris or a Hitchens, but atheism has been in trouble for some time, and their arguments against religion will not solve its problem. Something more than arguing against religion is needed. Not a substitute religion, but a more or less coherent picture of our world and our place within it. We need contemporary ways of orienting ourselves and our societal life—individual and collective starting points and first principles.

Secularists are not flourishing because we lack coherent

philosophies that effectively answer today's vital life questions. The person who puts his finger on our problem is an enemy of disbelief, Oxford theologian and Anglican priest Alister McGrath. He points to today's revival of religion in the United States and elsewhere as indicating, in contrast with atheism, religion's "life-enhancing and identity-giving power," especially when it "anchors itself in the hearts and minds of ordinary people, is sensitive to their needs and concerns, and offers them a better future." Atheism's appeal to the human imagination had once been a powerful draw which, McGrath says, has long since shown itself intellectually bankrupt. Moreover, he believes that atheism was politically implicated in Communist governments' efforts to suppress religion, and by a leap of logic, he lays all of Communism's failures and crimes at the feet of atheism. Once the "established religion of modernity," atheism today shows itself to McGrath as a "shopworn, jaded, and tired belief system."

In this account, McGrath reverses Ingersoll: 125 years on, it is religious belief that is alive and forward-looking, while disbelief "now lacks the vitality that once gave it power." But what specifically has declined within atheism and in its relationship to our world? Working our way through McGrath's book-length narrative, we repeatedly encounter "sunset" and "twilight" metaphors, which convey to us the feeling that disbelief in God has grown "old." More than actual analysis, this is intimidation by trendiness. Very much as with postmodernism, from which McGrath draws his key weapon (built into its name), we again and again sense his sweeping dismissal of modernity as being "over." In this postmodern world, McGrath seems to be saying, religion has once again come into vogue and irreligion has gone out of style.

Yet despite an almost total absence of close argument or historical analysis, McGrath does successfully manage to tap a widespread feeling that atheism, once so vibrant and self-confident, no longer seems to be on the cutting edge of today's world. What makes McGrath's kind of "history" seem so plausible today is that he forces us to confront the sense that atheism has not kept up with the world's changes, has in some way become old-fashioned. Above all, he forces us to acknowledge the passing of Enlightenment confidence that was built into modern disbelief. The strongest underpinning throughout most of atheism's history, its faith in Progress, has become atheism's fatal flaw.

The Enlightenment vision, after all, was that material, social, political, and intellectual progress was caused by, and would in turn encourage, the waning of religion. Ingersoll intimated that humans, acting on their own independently of religion and God, were becoming wiser and making vast technological, economic, political, and moral advances—secularization and progress were going hand in hand. Ironically, in the writings of Auguste Comte and Herbert Spencer that did so much to implant the idea of Progress in nineteenth-century minds, Progress became a substitute religion. Comte transformed it into a full-fledged law of history and then "social Darwinist" Spencer elevated it into a law of nature. Belief that historical or natural forces were inevitably making life better gave many people hope and comfort, as religion once did.

Were the *philosophes* and those who followed them being unreasonable in believing this? It was not a crazy vision. During the nineteenth century, the industrial revolution, spurred and nurtured by a spirit of calculation and yielding a dazzling array of techniques, inventions, projects, and goods, did in fact lead people to focus expectantly on the human, the here and now, and the earthly rather than a heavenly future.

But while the twentieth century in many ways confirmed the belief in Progress as human betterment, it also cruelly mocked it in others. Dazzling technologies, amazing increases in productivity, a cult of innovation, and waves of emancipation all did happen, but so did sheer destruction on a scale scarcely imagined by earlier centuries, notably over one hundred million people killed in foreign and civil wars and genocide. The accumulated weight finally made itself felt—of the Holocaust, Stalinism, and other catastrophes and threats. Meanwhile, modern economies and social systems grew adept at replacing traditional insecurities with thoroughly contemporary ones—to take only one example, lives are dominated by the "bottom line" that closes factories and moves jobs overseas. Small wonder that, in the last few years of the twentieth century, writers such as Foucault, Lyotard, and Derrida, calling themselves or dubbed "postmodernists," delivered sweeping postmortems on the "grand narratives" of Progress, Marxism, and other characteristically modern outlooks, as well as on modernity itself.

At New Year's, 2000, the waning of modern optimism could be summed up in a striking contrast: between the mood of hopeful anticipation that had accompanied the turn of the twentieth century, and the dazzling but empty media spectacles ushering in a new millennium crowded by fear of the Y2K breakdown. By now it has become regarded more as a sign of naiveté than anything else to wax enthusiastic about Progress, and fewer and fewer in the advanced world still anticipate their children's lives becoming better than their own. We all know: There is no force operating to make the world better. No longer hitched to the star of Progress, atheism, agnosticism, and secularism have lost conviction and optimism, and thus a main source of their missionary energy.

My reader may sense this in her own self-doubt. During the

Golden Age of free thought, the denial of God's existence was linked with a worldview that gave people a sense of meaning, direction, belonging, and purpose. However, it provided bearings far too easily: if, as so many unbelievers were convinced, religion was a consoling substitute for a sorry life on earth, a quasi-religion of Progress came to substitute for the comforts once provided by religion.

Given the eclipse of progress, secularists are today faced with a task more daunting than that of attacking religion: the need to develop meaningful secular worldviews that are no longer explicitly or implicitly tied to the belief in human and societal advancement.

Given our recent public wave of American piety, it is difficult for an unbeliever today to feel as if she is on the cutting edge of this society. But if not riding atop the wave of history, she still represents a significant trend both in the United States and in the world. She will certainly be helped to find her voice by the "breaking the spell" accomplished by Harris, Dennett, Hitchens, and Dawkins. But she needs more than systematic attacks on, and analyses of, religion.

My reader starts out today with the link broken between her own secular life and the optimistic and coherent outlook that once encouraged previous generations. What might any of the other great freethinkers find to say today, their confidence in the future destroyed by historical developments? What would Robert Ingersoll sound like today, deprived of his faith that the secularizing world was going to be a better world, no longer able to believe in "the angel of Progress," deprived of his soaring sense of life's meaning, deprived of the hope that knowledge and freedom from superstition are the keys to a truly human future? Even if he might be shown European secularization as a sign of human improvement, he would be forced to admit that this stems from, rather than energizes, material and social betterment. Moreover, his faith in human reason, science, and technology is no longer so firmly shared in today's secularized world. Its very capacities that helped produce over one hundred million deaths in the twentieth century now arguably usurp the place once accorded to God, by becoming able to end human life itself. We may have "conquered the dark" in Susan Jacoby's wonderful phrase, but our own deeper darkness, assisted by human reason, is now threatening around every corner.

It is no wonder that in Europe, the terrain of so many refutations of Progress, where secularists are paradoxically not on the defensive, many countries are simultaneously becoming both postreligious societies and post-Progress societies, believing very little in either. Religious indifference may be slowly replacing belief because a secure existence has been slowly replacing the struggle for survival, but questions about the meaning of a life without God remain on the agenda. In France strong mainstream voices on the right such as Luc Ferry (former minister of education), and, on the left, such as philosopher Michel Onfray, are writing for a wide audience and interpreting living without God as a positive and intellectually coherent undertaking.

With them, the moment we leave the debates over religion and ask what we ourselves believe, we find ourselves entering into a rich and exciting terrain. We look ahead to the future by returning to Immanuel Kant's three great questions: What can I know? What should I do? What may I hope? Today, these translate into several twenty-first-century questions driving the several chapters that follow. Given our contemporary understandings of the universe, what is our place in the world and our sense of life's meaning? What happens to our sense of individual responsibility for our world and our own lives as we become increasingly aware of the immensity of the social, natural, and psychological forces imposing themselves on us, and the complexity of the systems to which we belong? As knowledge and expertise proliferate exponentially, what has become of our confidence in education, our faith in our understanding, and our democratic belief in the power of citizenship? How do we face dying today, and what does death mean for a life without God? And taking all of these together and bringing Kant up to date, is there reason to hope today? Answering these questions is the central task of a twenty-first-century secular philosophy.

Gratitude

HIKING THROUGH A NEARBY WOODS ON A SPRING DAY
recently, I followed the turning path and suddenly saw a tiny
lake, then walked down a hill to its edge as birds chirped and
darted about, stopping at a clearing to register the warmth of
the sun against my face. Feelings welled up: physical pleasure,
delight in the sounds and sights, gladness to be out here on this
day. But something else as well, curious and less distinct, a vague
feeling more like gratitude than anything else but not toward any
being or person I could recognize. Only half-formed, this feeling
didn't fit into any familiar category, evading my usual lenses and
language of perception.

This is because giving thanks, central to Judaism, Christianity,
and Islam, is virtually absent from our secular culture. But this
deprives those who live without God of much of life's coherence
and meaning. For there is much to be grateful for. Exploring this
little-noticed feeling and idea from a secular point of view opens
a new way of experiencing our relationship with forces, entities,
and beings beyond our individual selves.

For many people, the one immediately available way of

experiencing my incipient feeling begins with thanking God. Religion provides a ready stock of lenses and language to iden- tify such experiences, because much of religion revolves around gratitude. Orthodox Jews, for example, thank God dozens of times a day, both in formal prayer and in common expressions: for the sunrise, for waking up alive, for food and drink, for going and coming safely, for every pleasure great and small, for health, for completing the day's activities, for nightfall, for sleep.

This way of relating to our lives and world has undeniable power. Hundreds of years after the beginning of modern science and seeing the world's disenchantment, it is still appealing to experience the natural and the human as expressing intentions of a higher being whom we seek to propitiate and influence— rather than consisting of processes understandable according to scientifically ascertainable laws. Moreover, thanking God out here on the trail would tie together everything I see and experience, direct me toward its ostensible source, and give me a personal relationship with that being. And it would unite my feeling of pleasure with my understanding, and fill me with a sense of gratitude that could point toward my life's meaning and its purpose.

Living without a supernatural being rules out this sense of enchantment and its responses and rituals of gratitude. Starting from a godless universe, wasn't Albert Camus right to begin *The Myth of Sisyphus* haunted by the otherness of a world unable to be reduced to human terms? He demanded that we confront our mortality, and the fact that our reason's demand for clarity can never be fully satisfied. The hope that we may live forever, and the hope that we can overcome the world's ultimate incoherence, is bound to be defeated. Our lives must always be absurd. The best we can do with a disillusioned life that resembles pushing a rock up a mountain is to be fully aware of our limits, and to live wholly within them. In these respects Camus went much further than Jean-Paul Sartre, who also began with absurdity but whom it affected less deeply. Sartre immediately looked beyond absurdity to human-imposed order, meaning, and purpose. But neither writer resembled those today who, troubled by the enormous odds against Earth winding up at the exact distance from our sun to make life possible, or pondering the statistical improbability of our own individual conception, conclude, with molecular biologist Robert Pollack, that science reduces us to no "more than numbers in a cosmic lottery with no paymaster."

Perhaps Camus tolerated the absurdity only because, like Meursault in *The Stranger*, he could stretch out on the beach and feel the sun's heat on his body. His writing brings home these experiences of nature with a force equal to his description of Sisyphus. Warmed by the sun, feeling no intention and no *being* behind it, he leaves us with intense momentary pleasures and Sisyphus's no less intense awareness of our limits and our fate. But do we have any deeper connection with our world? After all, as we learn from the handful of secular Western writers who have touched upon the topic of gratitude, how can we be grateful to what has no mind and no will—for example, the sun itself?

But we need not become Sisyphus, heroically resigned to a life devoid of ultimate meaning—or whose meaning lies in his intense consciousness of being alive and doomed to die. Nor need we assert the absurdity of a world that does not manifest God's will, by proclaiming that science reveals nothing but a "cosmic lottery." Scientific rigor does not exclude meaning. Think after all of the sun's warmth. The sun is a force that makes possible nature as we know it, including all plant and animal life, indeed our very existence. It intends nothing, least of all toward us personally, but its warmth on our face means, and tells us, and gives us, a great deal. Whatever he asserted in *The*

Myth of Sisyphus, Camus's powerful sense of the sun suggests that he understood implicitly that all life on Earth, we human beings included, exists daily in relation to this source of warmth and light. We *are* because of, and in our own millennial adaptation to, such fundamental forces, and all living things have evolved in relation to the universe, solar system, and Earth, in precisely those ways that make human life possible. We belong to an order, a life system, which, however blind and indifferent to us as individuals, gives us our collective and individual possibilities.

Such scientific facts contain immense philosophical significance. At the very least, the structures and processes studied by science make it unseemly to thank a personal God for intervening to cause the pleasures of my hike, and my feeling of well-being makes a mockery of the notion of cosmic absurdity. Astronomy, physics, chemistry, and biology tell us that my moment of gratitude while hiking opens a window of awareness into some of our most intimate yet impersonal relationships with the cosmic and natural forces and processes that make us possible. Our (or Meursault's) subjective reasons for taking pleasure in the sun are linked to objective facts: the life-giving properties of its precise range of warmth and its exact amount of light. It is near enough to Earth but not too near, far enough from it but not too far. Any greater or lesser distance would make it too cold or too hot to sustain life.

The sights and sounds that delight us are also keyed to and determined by the sun. Green leaves as far as the eye can see are part of the life-sustaining process of photosynthesis, which uses the sunlight, carbon dioxide, and water to create both the energy that fuels living things and the oxygen of the atmosphere. We dwell in and breathe the oxygen, are made of water and Earth's other elements, and consume living things in order to survive, as they do each other. But all this happens only because we all possess the very same chemical, physical, and biological structures. This is made more, not less true, by the struggle for survival among individuals and between species. As Charles Darwin wrote in *On the Origin of Species,* "the structure of every organic being is related, in the most essential yet often hidden manner, to that of all other organic beings, with which it comes into competition for food or residence, or from which it has to escape, or on which it preys." If, as he says, "all living things have much in common, in their chemical composition, their germinal vesicles, their cellular structure, and their laws of growth and reproduction," it is for the simplest of reasons—common descent, taking place over more than three billion years. All plant and animal species have evolved from "one primordial form," a common ancestor, single-cell eukaryotes. Evolutionary science since Darwin has been confirming how, in his words, "species have changed and are still slowly changing by the preservation and accumulation of successive slight favorable transitions."

In *The Myth of Sisyphus* Camus powerfully conveys a mood of absurdity, and he wisely roots it in our subjective longing, not in the world itself. After Darwin, we might imagine a universe that is truly absurd—for example, one where humans, plants, and animals have nothing in common and are unable to nourish each other. But the image flickers out, because it is impossible to even imagine how such a world would support life. Laboring instead to understand the many similarities and interconnections of the real world, Darwin was led by his studies to delight in its order and coherence. His descriptions help explain my own gratitude:

> It is a truly wonderful fact—the wonder of which we are apt to overlook from familiarity—that all animals and all plants throughout all time and space should be related to each other in group subordinate to group, in the manner which we everywhere

behold—namely, varieties of the same species most closely related together, species of the same genus less closely and unequally related together, forming sections and subgenera, species of distinct genera much less closely related, and genera related in different degrees, forming sub-families, families, orders, subclasses, and classes.

One of the great pleasures of reading Darwin is that his general conclusions are drawn from specific research, which he always presents with admirable clarity. Here is how he describes the relationship of the structures of different organic beings in competition with, and in relation to, others:

> [I]n the beautifully plumed seed of the dandelion, and in the flattened and fringed legs of the water-beetle, the relation seems at first confined to the elements of air and water. Yet the advantage of plumed seeds no doubt stands in the closest relation to the land being already thickly clothed by other plants; so that the seeds may be widely distributed and fall on unoccupied ground. In the water-beetle, the structure of its legs, so well adapted for diving, allows it to compete with other aquatic insects, to hunt for its own prey, and to escape serving as prey to other animals.

To describe how species live in relation to each other, Darwin tells about his experiments to determine how a certain variety of bees fertilize red clover. Mice destroy the bees' nests and honeycombs, except near towns and villages where cats destroy the mice. "Hence it is quite credible that the presence of a feline animal in large numbers in a district might determine, through the intervention first of mice and then of bees, the frequency of certain flowers in that district." In explaining nature's diversity, he tells us about studying "a piece of turf, three feet by four in size" which was subjected to the very same conditions for a number of years and "supported twenty species of plants, and these belonged to eighteen genera and to eight orders." Evolution is co-evolution: "Thus I can understand how a flower and a bee might slowly become, either simultaneously or one after the other, modified and adapted in the most perfect manner to each other, by the continued preservation of individuals presenting mutual and slightly favourable deviations of structure."

How can our sense of life's meaning not be affected by Darwin? Think of his stress on evolution entailing slight adaptations for the sake of survival, in a process of co-evolution under competitive conditions, and taking place over vast periods of time. This is especially so when his summary of what happens during evolution concludes not that the world was created for us, but the opposite. If "all the organic beings which have ever lived on this earth have descended from some one primordial form, into which life was first breathed," then our own evolution through natural selection has entailed hundreds of millions of years of adaptation to physical, chemical, biological, and climatological conditions. Like every surviving species, from the worms in the soil to the songbirds that delight us, from the bacteria in our stomachs to the mites on our pillows, we have evolved so as to be uniquely fitted to our place in the environment.

Now, it may seem appropriate to feel gratitude toward the sun, or even toward the plants that generate the atmosphere's oxygen, but toward microbes? Songbirds yes, but what about all the repulsive creatures we routinely avoid or ignore? Shouldn't we be no less thankful toward the bacteria in our stomachs than toward the rain? To insist on being consistent toward "all things great and small," shouldn't we be saying hosannas to earthworms?

If gratitude is no more than an emotion, felt wholly subjectively and at moments of personal well-being and pleasure, then we lose nothing by ignoring the microbes, bacteria, and earthworms. If it is wholly up to us to choose whatever we feel thankful toward, stretching or limiting our gratitude is entirely arbitrary. Then it scarcely matters what or who we thank, what beings we devise to feel grateful toward. Feelings of gratitude would invariably be imprecise, and even vague and fuzzy.

For example, M. J. Ryan, editor of the *Random Acts of Kindness* series, a best-seller of the early 1990s, followed up with *Attitudes of Gratitude*. In this book Ryan promotes gratitude as a kind of self-help. A grateful attitude cures perfectionism, makes us feel good about ourselves, makes us healthier, eliminates worry, allows us to live in the present and accept what we have, and attracts people to us. "As we give thanks, our spirits join with the Great Spirit in the dance of life that is the interplay between giver and receiver." With cloying self-satisfaction, Ryan asserts vague links to the rest of the universe without a hint of Darwin's scientific determination to understand what these might really be.

This manual of secular gratitude suggests why, aside from holy books, past writings on gratitude are so few and far between— Seneca, Hobbes, Adam Smith, Simmel. It may be a common emotion, but it has been difficult to pin down. These authors are concerned with being precise, focusing on person-to-person encounters with actual gift-givers and benefactors, occasionally generalizing a bit to society as a whole. According to Smith, for example, to be a "complete and proper" object of our gratitude, something must not only be "the cause of our pleasure, but it must also be capable of feeling" this sensation and have produced it in us "from design." While we may feel gratitude toward objects or animals, strictly speaking these are not appropriate objects. This is probably why in a recent interview philosopher Daniel Dennett longed, tongue in cheek no doubt, for someone to thank for the universe. Or why an early draft of this chapter appeared in a number of publications, including the *Toronto Star*, as "Thank Who Very Much?" And it is also why, 250 years earlier,

Adam Smith was somewhat perplexed to note his own gratitude toward inanimate objects such as a comforting snuffbox, useful penknife, or trusty walking staff.

Since I discern no more intention behind the sun, the hiking trail, and the lake, don't my quasi-feelings of appreciation, like Smith's, deserve to stay mute? Even if such impulses are inevitable, as Dennett and Smith suggest, aren't they crude and even childlike? As some philosopher friends insist, these are wholly subjective, because they lack a demonstrable, structural connection with any sources of such feelings. I may feel gratitude strongly, like Ryan, but this may say more about my own mood than anything else. My feelings might be no more than a vestige of what philosopher Julian Baggini, drawing on Freud's analysis of religion, calls the period before "we cast off the innocence of supernatural world views." Once we have grown out of projecting onto the world "benevolent parents who will look after us," perhaps we'll stop anthropomorphizing objects and natural processes.

But the feeling persists, and remains strong. On his forty-fourth birthday Nietzsche proclaimed: "On this perfect day, when everything is ripening, and not only the grape turns brown, the eye of the sun just fell on my life: I looked back, I looked forward, and never saw so many and such good things at once ... *How could I fail to be grateful to my whole life? ...*" Responding to Nietzsche, philosopher Robert Solomon asks, "If one does not believe in God, how can one be grateful for life and all of its blessings?" Solomon answers that we should sever gratitude from interpersonal emotions and think of what we owe to larger and impersonal forces, while at the same time avoid the "limp" solution of "being grateful 'to the universe.'" Doing so would lead us to glimpse "the bigger picture." Solomon's point, like Nietzsche's, is to *become aware* "of one's whole life, being reflective in a way that most of us are not, most of the time." He does not advocate saying hosannas to microbes, but rather acknowledging "we are always vulnerable and dependent beings."

Solomon helps us realize that our sense of gratitude needs to be educated, and in what direction, by focusing on our vulnerability and dependence. One need not read too far in *The Origin of Species* to be reminded of both. Remarkably enough, the paragraph where Darwin introduces the "Struggle for Existence" mentions a collateral theme no less than three times: *dependence*. Darwin begins by indicating that we misunderstand nature completely when we focus exclusively on its abundance and ignore that the songbirds we so enjoy are "constantly destroying life" to survive. They too, "or their eggs, or their nestlings," are constantly being destroyed. But he understands "the term 'Struggle for Existence' in a large and metaphorical sense, including dependence of one being on another." This includes a plant's dependence on moisture and mistletoe's dependence on birds for the dissemination of its seeds.

As we watch Darwin lay out his master theme of universal competition, we may ask why he didn't reverse the order, to prioritize dependence, or at least give it equal weight. After all, both competition and dependence are essential in biology. Darwin was, first of all, determined to puncture any Panglossian or religion-inspired myth of happy and harmonious nature. This may have led him to stress competition over dependence when discussing the relationships of individuals and species. And there is a second likely reason: he sought to account for the immense profusion of seeds and eggs and young created by every living thing seeking to reproduce itself, the vast majority of which do not survive. At the very outset of *The Origin of Species* Darwin remarks that a pair of ducks will produce seven or eight ducklings every year, both as a result and a cause of the universal struggle. Perhaps two of these ducklings will survive to reproduce, and if so, the duck population will be fortunate enough to remain stable. After all, the slowest breeders of all—a pair of elephants—if unchecked by nature, might generate over fifteen million descendants in five hundred years! But competition is a cardinal fact of nature, and dependence is another name for the reality that the overwhelming proportion of this profusion not only fails to reproduce but becomes consumed in one way or another by the few surviving plants and animals.

Universal interdependence: this is the other side of the struggle for survival. Which leads us to another reason why Darwin did not grant it equal status. In mid-nineteenth-century Britain the struggle for survival, not universal interdependence, was in the air. Herbert Spencer's formulation, "the survival of the fittest," became the popular slogan, as Spencer said, for "that which Mr. Darwin has called 'natural selection, or the preservation of favoured races in the struggle for life.'" Successful ideological campaigns portrayed the "favoured races," the economic and social victors and colonial rulers as the "fittest," and the social order as a natural order. A wealthy landowner writing during the high tide of industrial capitalism and imperialism, Darwin found this construction of his work to be a natural one, and in the 1869 edition of *On the Origin of Species* he not only gave Spencer credit but himself spoke of "Natural Selection, or the Survival of the Fittest." He embraced this formulation of his ideas even while as a scientist he continued to stress the processes of competition and selection and the relationships of interdependence.

Today we can sidestep the ideology and follow him in this direction. Spurred by both Solomon and Darwin, we can better educate ourselves about objective processes and relationships that stir our gratitude. We can see how these are structures of our world and not just needs of our psyche. This often happens when people experience the wilderness. They are awakened to their relationship to the universe, the earth, plant and animal life, the seasons, and themselves as natural beings. In a fascinating film by Christopher Barns, Doug Hawes-Davis, and Drury Gunn Carr, *American Values, American Wilderness,* a number of people speak about their experience of being in the wilderness. Something profound happens to them as they sense themselves in the vastness of the earth, nature, and the wider universe, feel connected with and at peace with themselves, and discover themselves rooted in a distant past. A common response is the determination to preserve the wilderness, and thus the possibility of such an experience for their children or grandchildren, and as their sense of time expands, even those living in the distant future. Other striking responses are a democratic sense—the belief that this heritage belongs to everyone and the desire to preserve this for everyone—and a feeling of this stewardship giving their life a meaning and purpose.

I returned to the hiking trail in midafternoon in summer, when insects were everywhere and birds were quiet, and the ground was soft from June rains. Although the temperature was only in the mid-seventies, the humidity made the air thick and hot. Flies buzzed around as I sweated, and I had to swat at mosquitoes. I was not moved to feel gratitude to worms and microbes in the soft ground or flies or mosquitoes, although I did have the hiker's feeling of being close to nature.

Is the natural order an indifferent one? Darwin, of course, stressed the struggle for survival, and described in detail the universal competition that forms every natural being's environment. This made him aware of such horrors as the ichneumon wasp, whose larvae parasitically live on paralyzed host insects, devouring them bit by bit but not attacking their hearts or vital organs until everything else is eaten. As Stephen Jay Gould says, this reminds us that nature does not contain "all things bright and beautiful" but is rather "replete with behaviors that our moral traditions would label as ugly and cruel." Yet Darwin, second to none in his sensitivity to competition and cruelty, famously ended *The Origin of Species* as follows:

> Thus, from the war of nature, from famine and death, the most exalted object which we are capable of conceiving, namely, the production of the higher animals, directly follows. There is grandeur in this view of life, with its several powers, having been originally breathed into a few forms or into one; and that, whilst this planet has gone cycling on according to the fixed law of gravity, from so simple a beginning endless forms most beautiful and most wonderful have been, and are being, evolved.

It is striking to realize that we, human beings, are one of nature's end products. And that we have evolved, through natural selection, in relation to the rest of nature, and with the brain capacity and disposition to understand and transform it. Nature may be indifferent to us, if such a word makes sense for what cannot think, but our survival by depending on it and understanding and consuming it, indicates that evolution contains a profound meaning—human life. This may not be, as Voltaire's Dr. Pangloss said, the best of all possible worlds, and there is no reason to believe, as many religious believers do, it is fashioned for us by God. But one of life's most open secrets is that we are part of nature. We are human creatures. Our many ways of depending are many reasons to be grateful—not only on nature's processes that we sense hiking in the woods, but also on cosmic forces and eons of history of plants and animals.

Allowing our relationships with nature to be mapped across time, from the big bang that created the sun, to the cosmic processes that created the earth, to the rains that created its oceans—yes, to the microbes in the water and in the soil, leading to the evolution of the other species of plants and animals—leads us to educate our sense of gratitude by becoming aware of our own sources. At the same time, we can sensitize ourselves to the vast impersonal forces and processes that make us possible. In other words we need not be grateful *to* any being for our place in nature, even though we are grateful *for* it. Glimpsing the larger picture means sensing that we humans have evolved in relation to all of this. We belong to it. Taken together, the universe, the solar system, and the natural and physical environment have created and continue to support—us.

But concluding here is to open only one eye. This is only part of the story of our dependence, and our gratitude. How is it that I am able to spend this day out on the trail, hiking, musing about these things? How did such a place come to exist, and how is it that I can partake of it, hiking from Pickerel Lake, Dexter Township, Michigan, past Dead Lake and on to Blind Lake? Everything and everyone has a story. These eleven thousand acres were set aside by the Department of Natural Resources of the State of Michigan as the Pinckney Recreation Area, a short distance from Ann Arbor and about an hour from Detroit. Other states and countries have many such parks, and like this one, many of them are near enough to population centers that millions of people have access to them. They too might possibly feel grateful for such publicly created and financed amenities.

The public history that created the park, and the sociological and economic facts that make it available, intersect with my own family and personal history. For the kind of job that gives me the freedom to come here I am indebted to my family, my wife, her family, and the Jewish environment of my childhood, as well as the existence of a public university in downtown Detroit, and a graduate program, now defunct, at Brandeis University where I could develop my intellectual interests and skills in the history of ideas. To that I must add the existence of collective bargaining at Wayne State University, which would never have come about without Detroit's massive automobile unions, and. . . .

Obviously, in sketching our own personal maps of gratitude, we come back to the "hosannas to microbes" problem: any full story, articulating every detail, becoming fully aware of all that we owe and to whom, is always *too* long. And its history includes generations, those who perpetuated our family line and demanded and achieved for themselves and those who would follow. Acknowledging this also means nodding to the collective processes and movements to which those who came before us belonged, including religious, ethnic, national, and class struggles in which they gained dignity, and even a measure of well-being. But it remains no less important to register more recent historical reasons why I'm able to be here, including the decision of my father's father and mother to leave Ukraine in 1885 and emigrate to the United States, and my mother's father's and stepmother's decision to emigrate from Galicia in 1913. Like the sun's heat, these decisions were not a moment too late or too soon: my grandparents left places of danger and made possible their children's and grandchildren's ability to lay claim to some of the opportunities offered by America in general and the existence of the automobile industry in Detroit in particular.

Every generation, and every individual, is situated within human history and its vast network of historically created skills and structures and processes and institutions, which constitute the nonbiological infrastructure of human life. We only become human by a long process of being raised within it, developing consciousness, language, fundamental skills, and gaining access to its specific tools, environments, and culture. Whoever and wherever we are, we start from wherever those who came before left off. It is no less profound for being a truism: all of this history is indeed *our* story. It becomes our very identity, not only consciously as our ideas, our self-awareness, and our specific expectations, but right down to and including how we stand, walk, talk, and feel. However complex and long is this our tale, it *can* be told. To describe our own detailed history is to sketch our own map of historical dependence.

Our social dependence not only reaches into the past, and the most basic steps of humans creating themselves, but is alive at every moment in the present. Our daily survival and functioning depend on dozens, hundreds, thousands of links. We belong to family and to all the obvious structures, networks, and processes—of work, friends, neighborhood, city, and nation (as well as the natural environment)—and to a social universe of which we usually remain unconscious. If we train our awareness on how structures and networks and processes are actualized around the world, we will eventually notice those whose work daily makes us and our lives possible, just as our work in some small way contributes to making them and their lives possible—our interdependence. My being on the hiking trail today suggests a vast human map in the present, drawing its colors from infrastructures and technologies, economic and social structures, and all the individual actions these guide and regulate.

Margaret Thatcher famously said: "There is no society, only individuals." She was wrong. In reality we live in an interdependent global society—to partake, just turn on the computer and "visit" the Internet—but as Thatcher's myopia demonstrates, unfortunately our dizzyingly complex interactions do not necessarily foster social awareness. The dominant practices of the global economy emphasize individual responsibility, personal initiative, and the centrality of "private" economic activity. Martha Albertson Fineman has written penetratingly about the "autonomy myth" that hides Americans' dependence on each other and on society. The more interdependent each person in the world becomes, paradoxically, the less social awareness of this there seems to be, and the more individuals locate themselves in the areas they can control personally. But even if it is lived passively and in a private corner, we live a collective life—even watching endless news, commentary, entertainment, and advertising on our own television in our own home is still a way of experiencing membership in the wider world.

Today more than ever such belonging connects us from the local to the global. Buying a Zulu Ilala palm basket sold at the beachfront in Durban, South Africa, puts its maker in our life and us in hers. Just notice our food from Peru and Mexico and Australia and a dozen regions of the United States; our clothing from Albania, Macau, and Mauritius, Honduras, Poland, and Sri Lanka; our household objects from China, Vietnam, South Africa, and Kenya. Another truism, also no less profound for this: In our survival and every activity we are utterly dependent on people, relationships, and structures across the world, and these can be mapped.

But thinking of the basket weaver in South Africa, I see two problems with this picture. It may seem noble to feel gratitude toward the sun, or toward members of our family, but in the scheme of understanding isn't a basket weaver in South Africa somewhat like a microbe in the soil? That is, she is part of a network so vast that it scarcely pays to notice any one person's specific contribution—which she makes, as in so many cases, only under the duress of needing to scrape together enough to survive. We might say the same about a clothing cutter in Macau or a docker loading Honduran bananas or a call center agent in India. Or about millions of wholly indifferent and self-interested

industrial and commercial processes and individuals. Senti-
mentality aside, Adam Smith's appreciation of his snuffbox was
obviously far more concrete, but was it any less meaningful? Out
on the trail, mightn't I feel no less but no more toward my hiking
shoes, and toward those working in the factory in China that
assembled them?

Despite its daunting detail, the resulting historical and contemporary picture of our social dependence need not be drawn
in a way that is limp or fuzzy. We need not rest satisfied with the
vague generalities of an M. J. Ryan. Historians and biographers,
for example, learn how to limit, and then structure, stories—
which by their very nature are so complex as to defy telling—and
then tell them. In trying to explain the life of one single person, the French novelist Gustave Flaubert, Sartre accumulated
more pages (2922 in English) than Flaubert's entire collected
works—without ever getting as far as the author's masterpiece,
Madame Bovary. Sartre set out to answer the question "What can
we know about a person?" and he left us with an unfinished story.
Accordingly, our own goal is not to be complete, but above all to
become aware of the planes and layers of our dependence.

Multiplying these doesn't diminish, but only enriches, all that
we human creatures belong to and all that we owe. Each of our
own maps of dependence reaches out to the cosmos and back
to our solar system and planet, includes the physical features of
Earth that make life possible, and the physical, chemical, and
biological processes that have evolved in a way to make human
history possible. And each one reaches back through all of history, a history which has taken place as a constant struggle for
survival, as human evolution and development, as endless conflict and migration, as victories over want and oppression, and as
personal, family, local, regional, national, and ethnic histories.

And stretching across the present, each of us belongs to, is shaped by, a synchronic story in which we are part of today's world: its social, economic, and technical flows and structures, its billions of people.

A second major problem built into our belonging to human history and society is that we belong unequally. On that humid summer day, two cyclists passed me and I met one other hiker. Only the four of us sought out this place and found our way here. Were we the only ones in this metropolitan area of nearly five million people able to take the time and with the means to come here? A leisurely day in the woods, an hour's drive from home, is simply not available to most Americans, let alone the vast majority of the world's people. Certainly not to the basket weaver in South Africa—hiking for recreation would be the furthest thing from her mind, although she may trudge several miles a day for water and for work. In my own case, my parents' savings made it possible to buy a small year-round house adjoining the recreation area, and my job makes it possible to hike and think and work at the same time. It is a privilege.

We are vastly unequal beneficiaries of the long process of human self-development, having systematically unequal acquisitions: vocabulary, language, consciousness, and even our very expectations. And this inequality marks our relationships with nature. Inasmuch as the global division of labor is also a division of well-being, it is fair to say that I owe my own pleasures on the hiking trail to numerous less-fortunate humans, who are at this very moment performing the toil that makes it possible. Is "owe" even the right word, since they hardly gave it freely?

What effect does this inequality have on feelings of gratitude? If gratitude stems from awareness of our place in the large picture, its accurate mapping will simultaneously provoke guilt and resentment. Most people in the two dozen countries with the highest standard of living today live on a plane with the wealthiest people who have ever lived. And it is their societies, certainly not their own individual achievements, which make this possible. At the same time, our racial and national and class belongings, and the planet's uneven distribution of resources, assign oppression and poverty to most of the rest of humanity. Not that all of these peoples' homelands lack resources: ironically, having great natural wealth has often been a curse, leading to domination from overseas, subjection, and enslavement. Some of the most thriving areas—England, Europe, New England—have been relatively poor in natural resources. And some of the richest areas—the American South, Bolivia, the Congo—are today the poorest. Ironically, even nature conspires against people, insofar as it is unequally controlled and draws the most powerful to exploit it. This is not a matter of chance, and in this very precise sense, the world is not indifferent but hostile to those who are so marked.

Just as those of us gripped by the "autonomy myth" fail to see our dependence on society and on others, we may find ourselves unwilling or unable to notice the force and meaning of our unequal belonging to nature, history, and society. But to become fully aware of, and thus *live* our dependencies, we must become conscious of the privileges and debilities they assign to us. Does this transfigure our gratitude, overwhelming it with guilt and anger? For example, would this ruin a thanksgiving celebration?

After all, when we gather with friends and family for a holiday, feelings of gratitude flow spontaneously. We are glad to be together, pleased that we have come from far and near, glad for this special day and the special meal. If such feelings can be educated, as I have tried to show, at our holiday toast we can freely express their actual sources, both natural and social, in the past and in the present.

People are accustomed to a moment of shared gratitude. Giving thanks to all that is beyond us, but makes us possible, is a common need. It has traditionally pointed people in a religious direction, and so we may even lack the language for acknowledging our cosmic, natural, and worldly sources. But what happens if we try? In our warm, joyous, comfortable feeling, and the moment of well-being it generates, we can pause to be grateful— for natural forces that have made our own life, and this reunion, possible; for the remarkable congruence of humans and the natural world that enables us to survive; to our ancestors distant and recent and their struggles, whose labors have accumulated in the comforts we enjoy; and to countless other people, wherever they are, whose toil helped set the table at which we feast.

An entirely secular giving of thanks is possible and necessary, and if we're not shy about voicing it, it will find its own shape. In stumbling to do so, we'll notice some remarkable things. Reverence for the forces beyond ourselves, normally projected onto a deity, is no less deep for finding its actual sources, and our bond with each other need not be weakened by being expressed without reference to a supreme being. Celebrating in this way does something new for us. If we choose to experience our connectedness without seeing ourselves as God's children, we may find new, adult, ways of sensing our unity not only with each other, but also with the cosmos, nature, history, and the social and economic worlds of other people. What we belong to is always larger than ourselves, much larger, but being part of it, we contribute to it as well. Our gratitude toward who and what makes our coming together possible can give us a profound feeling of belonging to each other and to the universe, and a sense of strength in doing so. Instead of lending our power to a being above us and then asking for it to be lent back to us, we may be able to feel our power as drawn from, and connected to, all that we depend on.

The personal philosophical question "Who am I?" gets answered rather differently, and more fulsomely, if, abandoning the autonomy myth, and together with others, we are willing and able to see our specific belongings and express gratitude for them. We can imagine a freely invented secular ceremony that would honor this awareness. Beginning by avoiding all displacement and denial, in a full-throated way, with precision and in whatever detail we need—with our minds as well as our hearts—we might celebrate what makes us and our well-being possible. Prayer is not necessary, but gratitude is.

Giving thanks on a holiday, when it is clear-eyed and acknowledges the fullness of our dependency, need not avoid noticing the unfairness of deeply ingrained parts of our lives and our social world. Seeing this flows naturally from acknowledging our dependence and belonging. Gratitude, yes, can even be mixed with guilt and anger. For the moment, we choose to focus on the one part of our experience, on an aspect of our lives, all the while knowing that our world is the opposite of empty and mute both for good and for ill. In the good moments of our lives we routinely bracket wars, disease, famine, death and dying, oppression, and a thousand other pains and evils. We know that we cannot lead decent lives if we are obsessed by these or if we deny and do nothing about them. There are times for heartfelt and clear-sighted gratitude, when we take the opportunity to acknowledge our world as alive and giving to us. Afterward, we can begin to appreciate what it demands of us.

CHAPTER THREE

The World
on Our Shoulders

WHAT DOES OUR BELONGING TO NATURE, HISTORY, AND society require of us? Our guilt and resentment about inequality should lead us neither to making sweeping conclusions about the unfairness of life nor to seeking psychotherapy to ease our troubled feelings; rather, they make active demands on us that can only be called *moral*. They point to how our interdependence is structured by privileges and disabilities.

In my own case, this book has been written in a small suburban town, Huntington Woods, Michigan, midway between the shrinking Motor City, Detroit, and the calm splendor of Bloomfield Hills; I am situated between guilt induced by my own unearned privileges and resentment at how richly endowed others are compared to myself. Detroit is often on my mind because I was born there and I work there. I grew up during its prime as America's great manufacturing center, left, and then moved back in time to witness its decline to half of its former size, the loss of most of its automobile production, and its rise to a new status as America's poorest major city. Many of the residents in this largely African American city are trapped in the inequalities resulting from three hundred years of slavery and a century of systematic racism and legal racial segregation, even after generations of struggle that gave them full legal equality. They are frustrated by disinvestment, white flight, continuing poverty, school segregation, and housing and employment discrimination. Siding with them in their continuing struggle, wrestling with the heritage of racism, is, very simply, the moral thing to do.

Living without religion, I dare to speak of morality! The exclamation mark is dedicated to all those who express astonishment that unbelievers can be moral without God. A frequent paper topic among my students is precisely this: How is it possible to be moral without religion? Those who ask this usually come from the unexplored assumption that accepting the Ten Commandments as the word of God is essential for ethical behavior. The doubt that any other path exists is so widespread that our culture endlessly recycles the old saw imputed to Dostoevsky's *Brothers Karamazov*: If God does not exist then anything is possible.

The primary relationship in the Ten Commandments, freshly analyzed by Sam Harris in *Letter to a Christian Nation*, is between the individual and God. The first four commandments focus on this, followed by six rudimentary demands for good behavior common to every culture: for honoring one's parents, against murder, theft, adultery, lying, and envy. When God drops away from our lives, what becomes of our morality? Atheists, agnostics, and secular humanists are frequently pressed to show how they are able to keep the other six commandments without the strong presence of God. But accusations about who is and is not moral might just as easily start from the opposite direction. The point is not that unbelievers are less moral than religious believers, but rather that conventional religious belief is morally quite narrow. Its *Thou shalts* and *Thou shalt nots* leave most of the world's injustices untouched. The Ten Commandments do not prohibit slavery, for example. Focusing only on specific strands of individual behavior, those ten commandments have long been wholly compatible with unjust societies. Obeying them is no recipe for making either an individual or a society moral.

If we leave behind the Ten Commandments and the relationship with God at their core, we may discover that the preeminence of God has long obscured our primary relationship: our belonging to society. Morality would then not emanate from a supreme being, but rather from our own belonging to a world larger than ourselves. Our dependencies confer obligations upon us—these are built into being human. We may choose to ignore them, but to do this is to become deadened not only to our place in the wider world but to a part of ourselves. Being grateful is about seeking our links, our connections, our identity. This should lead to accepting our responsibilities toward all that makes us ourselves.

If there is any kind of ultimate lawgiver, it is our social being, simultaneously higher and more enduring than our individual self, and also its deepest source. Socrates paid homage to it in *Crito* when he refused to escape from his death sentence, saying such an action might encourage disrespect for the *polis* that had nourished him. This was a very early way in Western civilization of expressing our social interdependence. As individuals we have obligations to the community to which we belong, not only in some external way, but as community members: it *is* us and we *are* it. We don't live our uniquely individual lives *over here* and then make forays to the wider world *out there* from time to time. Belonging to society means that in our deepest individuality we are always living social lives, here, in this particular place.

———

So how am I, are other whites, responsible for the plight of black Americans, in Detroit or elsewhere, who have been unable to climb out of poverty? Working in the city where I was born, what do I have to do with the inherited inequalities of people I don't even know? In stating the issue in personal terms, I'm following the way it often gets posed, and answered. The late former congressman Henry Hyde, when confronted with the demand for reparations for slavery, replied, "I never owned a slave. I never oppressed anybody. I don't know that I should have to pay for someone who did [own slaves] generations before I was born." The objective formulations of the reparations claim say that it's nothing personal, but that America as a nation has a responsibility toward the descendants of people who were kept in bondage by state-sponsored slavery and then in second-class citizenship by state-sponsored segregation. As Randall Robinson said, clarifying the demand, "No one holds any living person responsible for slavery or the later century-plus of legal relegation of blacks to substandard education, exclusion from home ownership via restrictive covenants and redlining, or any of the myriad mechanisms for pushing blacks to the back of the line." Still, it would be an evasion to deny the personal dimension.

My grandfather and grandmother came to this country from Russia in 1885, over twenty years after Emancipation. How could they have had any responsibility for the plight of black Americans? I don't know about Congressman Hyde's family, but I have to admit that my immigrant grandparents, and then my parents, benefited personally from the segregation and peonage imposed on blacks for the next several generations. For one thing, my father and his father before him profited by not having to compete with black men for their livelihood. Segregation and racial discrimination sometimes boosted both men's odds of getting decent jobs by just enough to make a difference—say, one in ten—and each man's vote took on a greater weight to the extent that blacks were deprived of the vote. Furthermore, their families' lives were made easier by the cheap servant labor available to them. I remember an old black man named Eddie, who would come around regularly to empty the ashes from our furnace and do other chores, and my mother had the services of a black cleaning woman, Annie, who came in once a week to do housecleaning, washing, and ironing.

On a harder-to-specify level, socially and psychologically, my immigrant grandparents entered into a society where their white skin placed them as superior to black people just by being here, no matter how poor they themselves were. When my grandfather came over from Russia as a young cap-maker, he found that being a Jew was not only much less of a handicap here than in the Old Country, but that he had acquired a new status: he became white. Interestingly enough, the census records for 1910 show the family living cheek by jowl with blacks near downtown Detroit, and in one family memory my grandfather, by now owner of a small grocery store, was hit over the head by a black man carrying a bottle who was trying to rob the store.

In an extremely race-conscious city, my father showed no particular pride in his white status, no sense of superiority, and later on he even felt a contrarian pride at our being one of the last white families in the old neighborhood to sell their house and move to the edge of the city. He would tell stories about two incidents that marked him deeply. The first was a high school debate in which he was assigned the impossible task of defending slavery, but about which he could only remember his partner's chilling and heartfelt declamation: "They were born to serve." The second was an incident that happened while traveling down South, on a trip to New Orleans, with a fellow insurance salesman named Schuster in 1930. Driving through Alabama, Schuster abruptly stopped their car by a field, went up to a young black woman he had spotted, and demanded there and then that she have sex with him, which she did. Then the two men drove on. Telling the story thirty years later, my father was still astonished and horrified.

These are among the countless ways immigrants and their children lived America's unresolved heritage of slavery during the one hundred years afterward. Did each of these ways make them personally complicit in the racism built into American society? And to the extent that racism continues, are we in any way responsible for its present manifestations? I attended a high school in which one-third of the students were black, and we all cheered for our integrated sports teams. But outside of gym class and study hall, the vast majority of black kids were tracked away from the mostly Jewish college-bound white kids. They weren't our servants, but they certainly weren't regarded as our equals, and I am sure many of them experienced daily humiliation in being treated as inferior.

Fifty years later, a brilliantly organized reunion assembled four hundred graduates and spouses, including a significant proportion of black alumni. The people attending such events have usually done well for themselves. As the climax of the evening's program, a film was shown that had just been assembled from photographs, home movies, and memories. As faces, voices, and footage rolled by, it slowly became clear that they mostly belonged to the handful of kids who had dominated the school. With a couple of exceptions, all images and reminiscences were of and by whites, one of whom gushed, with great feeling, "We were family!" Listening to the 1950s black music loudly accompanying the images and playing softly behind the interviews, did the fifty or so African Americans watching, including some veterans of struggles for equality during the 1960s and 1970s, feel themselves marginalized once more? Did they experience the film as a slight? Did they see it as a result of racism, whether conscious or unconscious? Or would they have concluded that only whites had been well off enough fifty years ago to own home movie cameras, or to save their old snapshots—or that those who made the film simply couldn't find more than two blacks to interview? Why, I asked myself, didn't the organizers and producers have the sensitivity to insist on greater balance? I wondered what to do as I watched, what effect it would have if I broke into the celebratory mood with a critical comment. As it turned out, I grumbled to two or three close white friends, and felt terrible.

Personally, then, not only the immigrant grandfather and the father, but also the son, had all lived amidst the ongoing nightmare of black America and, I am sure, my grandchildren will continue to participate in what remains of it as they grow up. So it isn't far-fetched to contemplate the share of personal responsibility and even guilt that might belong to each of us. I may not have wronged anyone directly and personally, although I do painfully recall unthinkingly telling a racist joke in the locker room during high school gym class and being overheard by a black friend walking by. He was obviously hurt, and was under-standably never so friendly again—he wasn't at the reunion. But as an individual I have shared in the gains of racial inequality, and so I must ask: What is my responsibility for it? My question can be expanded to include not only ugly practices but also other forms of inequality, discrimination, and marginalization. What is my individual responsibility for this world to which I belong? And how should I assume it?

Living without God demands mapping my responsibilities accurately and assuming them consciously. This is difficult in a culture profoundly affected by religion, where confusion reigns about just what it means to take responsibility for anything. Among believers, such questions are often muddled by being posed within traditional frameworks of sin and grace—individual human actions cause our world's evils, only God can relieve us of their consequences, and that only ultimately. A key component of this psychic and moral drama is the fact that it usually erases institutional and social awareness: if the essential relationship is between myself and God, the essential moral question is about my own personal behavior vis-à-vis other individuals. In it we see ourselves primarily as separate individuals obeying or disobeying a handful of injunctions received from on high, a stance that renders us unable to concretely analyze most of the really significant moral issues of our lives.

We can get clearer on such questions by shifting drastically and turning to issues left over from the most cruel of human centuries, the last one. Who was responsible for the extermination of millions of Jews at places such as Auschwitz and Treblinka? This question opens out to more general ones. Don't the institutions and instruments of the modern world function increasingly to hide individuals from responsibility? How are ordinary citizens responsible for social evils that they may disagree with but are committed by their governments? How far can we extend the accusation of complicity with actions actually committed by a tiny handful or by destructive systems, practices, and habits that seem to perpetuate themselves, hanging on by a kind of inertia and lack of will to change them? Thinking about the Holocaust can allow insight into our own responsibility for the evils of our own society. Yet why are we still puzzling about responsibility for the Holocaust, over fifty years later—especially after mountains of documentation, writing, and films about this most infamous

of historical events have accumulated and become so promi-
nent in the public consciousness? Remarkably, great confusion
persists, even now, about what responsibility for it means and
exactly who was responsible.

According to the charter of the International Military Tribunal
at Nuremburg, "Leaders, organizers, instigators and accomplices
participating in the formulation or execution of a common plan
or conspiracy to commit [crimes against peace, war crimes, or
crimes against humanity] are responsible for all acts performed
by any persons in execution of such plan." As regards the Nazi
extermination program, a handful of people seem to have made
the policy and drawn up the plans to implement it. Their responsibility was obvious. Then tens of thousands executed it, but only
by obeying orders: are they not responsible in some way that the
Tribunal didn't consider? The SS guards brought to trial since,
such as Ivan "the Terrible" Demjanjuk, are usually only those
thought guilty of extreme brutality. The overwhelming majority
of the tens of thousands have lived out their lives peacefully in
the years since, declared not responsible by the Tribunal charter,
fearing neither apprehension nor judgment.

Beyond these, hundreds of thousands more participated as
indispensable parts of the machinery, making the extermina-
tions possible but never touching a living, or even a dead, victim.
Some handled the victims' eyeglasses or assayed their gold rings
and teeth; some inventoried their property or carefully recorded
their names and numbers. They would have denied responsibility even more vehemently than those who were exempted by the
Tribunal. And beyond the very careful and intelligent courtroom
discussions of the actual degree of culpability of the major actors
and the cruelest guards—a tiny circle—the world has felt no need
to further clarify just what it means to have been responsible
for the Holocaust. Clearly, the overwhelming majority of the

cogs in the wheels have lived on unnoticed, as if to confirm that, beyond the key Nazis and sadistic guards, no one else deserves to be brought to trial.

Yet we know that the web of responsibility for the Holocaust extends beyond those few who have been brought to trial. We were reminded, for example, by those relatives back from the war who refused for the rest of their lives to buy a German car. But was that going too far? Of course the German state has been deemed responsible, a burden taken on by the Federal Republic's decision to pay reparations to survivors and the state of Israel. But what about individual officials? Business enterprises? The hundreds of thousands, even millions of "good Germans" who made the Holocaust possible? Weren't they part of the web of institutional functioning, ideological support, and political complicity without which Jews and others could never have been annihilated? Intimately linked with that web, and permitting it to function, was the rest of German society, all those who, in philosopher Karl Jaspers' words, "went right on with their activities, undisturbed in their social life and amusements, as if nothing had happened." Has the Federal Republic paid the bill for all of its citizens?

All of these are peculiarly modern questions. Think about what they presuppose: a long historical process leading both to the emergence of the individual as ethical subject, and to the modern nation-state and its conception of citizenship as being a relationship between that ethical subject and the larger community. It is in today's world that this kind of responsibility becomes an issue, growing more intense as the society becomes more democratic. We see this relationship in equally modern ways: when soldiers deny responsibility for brutal acts that they have committed in wartime, ascribing them to the nation-state structures that placed them in the position to commit them or even

commanded them; and when individuals who themselves did
no direct harm are accused of supporting and making possible
the brutality of other individuals. In the first case, the individual
denies responsibility for an act she actually performed, dissoci-
ating herself from the consequences of her own act by claiming
that she was not acting as ethical subject but obeying an order
or carrying out her role. And in the second case the individual is
claimed to be responsible for an act she did *not* commit—because
in aiding and abetting it she in fact made it possible.

"I was only obeying orders" is the claim given to the first
question. The twentieth century's great philosopher of responsibility, Sartre, has sketched a sweeping, nonetheless effective,
reply: By choosing to obey them, I have made the orders, and
all acts springing from them, my own. The extermination-camp
guard always retains personal responsibility, and is free to evaluate whether orders are right or wrong, legal or illegal. By now
Sartre's argument on this point has largely won out. Since 1945
humanity collectively seems to have amplified the meaning of
citizenship by deciding that every individual serving any state
has the responsibility to subject its every order to the scrutiny of
conscience. From governments to military commands to political activists to philosophers, a kind of international consensus
has grown up—extending to the American war in Vietnam, the
struggle over Croatia and Bosnia, the military coup in Chile, the
Israeli army's treatment of Palestinians and Lebanese, and the
use of torture by Americans in Iraq—arguing that it is correct,
and necessary, for the individual conscience to evaluate orders
ethically before carrying them out. This reflects a growing sense
that the individual is responsible for every act she carries out as
part of a larger institution.

In living our daily lives, however, the second issue is both
more important and more muddled. "I was only a clerk." Or:

"I did not know it was happening." Or: "I opposed this war but was powerless to stop it." "I have no power to control what the politicians do." Or angrily: "It's *their* war." Or, in a slightly whiny tone: "What could *I* do?" Or "Black poverty isn't my fault." We are dealing with the issue of complicity, of ordinary citizens living their ordinary routines in societies that vary from unequal to oppressive, to brutal to criminal, from democratic to colonial to dictatorial.

One way to clarify attribution for events like the Holocaust or to current-day racism is to think in terms of a spiral of responsibility. The spiral moves outward from those most directly responsible to those indirectly responsible. It winds from those who conceived and ordered the Final Solution—Hitler and his closest associates—to those who acted on their behalf and planned and directed its every detail (historian Raul Hilberg lists about three hundred high officials and party leaders), to those who directly laid hold of Jews, shipped them to places like Auschwitz, and once there, placed them in the gas chambers (Hilberg estimates the number of these mostly Waffen-SS concentration-camp guards at about fifty thousand). There were in addition about ten thousand direct administrators of the process. All of these people acted as vital components of the machinery of destruction—to put it more sharply, they *were* the machinery of the Final Solution, each one occupying an essential post in the division of labor which alone made possible the extermination of European Jewry.

But how deeply does the spiral extend into Germany, how far beyond those who directly bloodied their hands? The next turn includes hundreds of thousands: not only the soldiers and SS troops who rounded up Jews and shipped them to the killing centers, but also those who expropriated their property, the clerks who catalogued it, the construction workers and railroad crews, the police, and administrative apparatus outside of camps that made possible the grisly work going on inside. As the spiral widens, it takes in those hundreds of thousands of government employees (who were required to be Nazi party members) supporting these actions by doing their job elsewhere in the division of labor, keeping the machinery of state running smoothly at hundreds of points. Beyond them was the Nazi party itself, which by 1933 had over two million members and once in power grew to over eight million. Then were those tens of millions of Germans outside the party who voted the Nazis into power (in the last election, in May 1933, the Nazis received 44% of the votes). These are joined on the spiral by millions more in the broad national consensus who supported Hitler's rearmament, which created jobs and ended the depression, and cheered Germany's aggressive foreign policy and imperial successes. And then we come to the outer turns of the spiral, where all those "good Germans" resided who, while disliking the Nazis and sensing the evil and madness of Hitler and of his movement, failed to do anything to block the Nazis' rise to power. Once Hitler was in power they may have continued to oppose silently and live in fear, but they also paid their taxes and gave themselves and their sons to the war effort.

We know today that the spiral does not end here. It continues beyond Germany, to those Allied leaders, and their administrators and political supporters, some of them Jewish, who knew about the extermination camps but had other priorities than pushing for their destruction. They did not cause the Holocaust, and perhaps were not what we usually regard as complicit in it; but they did not take action to stop it. "What else could they have done?" Ah, the question of questions! It may be asked of millions, bad people and good, who formed this particular spiral of responsibility. It took all of them to create and accept the conditions that led to the Holocaust. Each contributed in a specific and definite way, and was responsible in a specific and definite way. All of those who ordered it and planned it are responsible for it, and all of those who carried it out are responsible for it, and all those who accepted it and allowed the Holocaust to happen are responsible for it—but in different ways, and in different degrees. No matter how far we look, we never see more than a few key actors actually carrying out the Final Solution. Most of the sixty million Germans were accomplices to varying degrees, according to their roles. To call them accomplices tells us a great deal about how the modern nation-state operates. Once the Nazis controlled its machinery, they required only a relative handful of obedient servants to operate it. Hitler's main victory, unfolding over the ten years before January 1933, was to win power. This required the active or passive consent of tens of millions—the strength of some, the weakness of others, the frenzied energy of some, the detached support of others, the moment-to-moment planning of some, the resigned passivity of others, the street violence of some, the frightened withdrawal of others. Many of the accomplices may have done very little, or even nothing. Some only averted their eyes. But each did precisely what was needed.

In this sense, even when partial, responsibility is absolute. The average "good" German was certainly no more responsible for the Holocaust than the average "good" American for the near-destruction of Vietnam and then, a generation later, the disaster in Iraq. But no less. When people refuse their part and actively assume their responsibility, as did thousands of Danes when orders came to ship away the Jewish community of Denmark, the machine grinds to a halt. Danes withdrew their tacit approval, their passive compliance, and took responsibility for Danish Jewry—and saved them. Daring to dispel the murk of

passive acquiescence to evil, they sensed that actively responding to the crisis might change the situation dramatically. And it
did.

Obviously not everyone in American society was equally culpable for the Iraq disaster. Some opposed it fiercely, publicly,
and persistently. But just as certainly it can be laid at the door
of more than a handful of neoconservative policymakers in the
White House and Department of Defense. Blaming only them
lets everyone off the hook who, by going along in a thousand
different ways, made it possible. If, in Nazi Germany, our gaze
extends beyond a handful of political leaders on the one hand
and brutal guards on the other, the destruction of Iraq was set
in motion by more than a few individuals in the vice president's
office and Defense Department, was carried out by more than a
few who committed abuses in the field. The accusation of complicity thus extends from the religiously conservative zealots
who mindlessly gave George W. Bush a blank check to invade a
foreign country not at war with, and not threatening, the United
States, to the political zealots delighted at the chance to reshape
the world in the American image, to the media cheering section
who sold the war to the American public, to the pusillanimous
Democratic politicians who feared the political fallout of not
going along—and includes all those who grumble but feel no
responsibility as citizens, as well as those who have withdrawn
from politics into completely private lives. They are all responsible, each in their own way.

Of course, the invasion of Iraq has not yet been declared a
crime, but it deserves to be. I mention it to show that our own
personal culpability for government actions is more of an issue,
not less, in a society as democratic and media-saturated as ours.
After all, our rulers, elected in massive public spectacles every

detail of which is "covered" many times over, make policy with obsessive attention to how it plays to the public. They act in our name. Anyone with eyes to see might have easily known, in the fall of 2002 and winter of 2003, that no credible evidence existed of an Iraqi threat to America. After all, there are few back rooms anymore where decisions can be made in secret, and in any case, truth outs quickly. Those who believed in the threat did so on blind faith, and they should be held responsible for that faith.

Either way, the American public's assent to this war was absolutely necessary for the war to occur, and the Bush Administration pulled out all the stops to secure it. Each and every one of us was targeted in this campaign, and those skeptics who used their minds and found their voices may have been overwhelmed by the yaysayers and intimidators and silenced, but they were right. We were all responsible for the war, and only a few of us opposed it, saying, "Not in our name."

The very fact that we can talk about responsibility for the war in Iraq seems to make it very different than racism in America today. Who is responsible for the kind of housing segregation that depends on the unavailability of decent alternatives? For school segregation that depends on residential patterns and city boundaries? For the fact that low-skill entry-level jobs pay poorly? For high levels of insecurity and unemployment among the uneducated? Many of the continuing inequalities between blacks and whites in America seem to be *nobody's fault*. They seem to be matters of history or inertia, no longer of choice or policy. What can *I* do about it?

As with many kinds of social inequality, whether or not we see clearly depends on a fundamental choice of perception: do we see ourselves as isolated, separate individuals, or instead recognize ourselves as belonging to, and depending on, a wider world? Do we acknowledge our own map of dependence? If we were to open our eyes wide enough to consciously live our individual lives as members of a local, national, and global society, we might care more about providing the chance for a decent life for every individual, including adequate healthcare, nutrition, and schools. Instead, Ten Commandments and all, we live in a moral universe that is ambivalent and ultimately incoherent about equality. We are all said to be equal politically and before the law, but socially and economically our individual worth varies enormously. Being "created equal" generates a powerful national impetus to equal citizenship rights for all. But how can we talk about equality of opportunity in a society marked by the greatest economic inequality of any advanced society? This is built into the American system: social and economic inequality, two of its hallmarks, make a mockery of the other, proud hallmark of American democracy, civic equality. Fair competition requires attention to our starting points, yet this is rare today as unequal schools, the rising costs of higher education, the growing gap in living conditions between well-off and poor—all solidify the prevailing unfairness.

Accepting responsibility for this means first acknowledging that we all belong to a community, as opposed to Margaret Thatcher's illusion that there are only individuals. The paradox of our time is that this kind of extreme individualism is riding high even while our interconnectedness is intensifying. The more interdependent each person in the world becomes, the less social awareness there seems to be. We are supposed to live our lives as if there were no community, as if each of us had become a Robinson Crusoe. But if, as I argue, "I" only exists within a "we," unless we look out for everyone else, no one is secure.

It is as members of society, as citizens, that our responsibility is the greatest. Being roused by guilt into individual acts of kindness may help a few individuals, but it leaves conditions unchanged. Social practices, structures, and policies can be altered, and social inertia can be overcome, only through widespread collective involvement as citizens. This may require active intervention on a dozen fronts, and it may require imaginative policies and even individual sacrifices. It is becoming harder to imagine because as the years of the New Deal and World War II become distant memories, awareness that Americans live in a community continues to fade, restored only momentarily by events such as 9/11 or during presidential elections.

Ignoring that we are interdependent is ruining our society. For one thing it makes it impossible to tackle any significant social problem. Decaying major cities, for example, are no longer rebuilt—they are abandoned or left to decay while awaiting investment. For another thing, the indifference corrodes us morally. For those who are well off, avoiding seeing their connection with those who live poorly coarsens their humanity.

Moral hardness is one personal consequence of ignoring inequality. Another is the demoralization from tolerating unfairness. A few may justify our scandalous inequality, many may just accept it because "life isn't fair," most will just ignore it—in each case, we worsen ourselves by this kind of complicity, by becoming indifferent to the wrong happening around us. Yes, inequality may be wholly impersonal, and we may have no intentional relationship to it, but by our failing to name it and confront it and do something about it, we wind up living by it. We make it ours. To condone and benefit from injustice is to become implicated in it. Just as they did in Nazi Germany.

Cynicism is irresponsibility masquerading as toughness: I struggled to get here, so why can't everyone else? Other people, and the world, are not my responsibility, but instead are tools

for my own well-being, or obstacles to be combated on my way
to a better life. Often we can hear anger in the cynic's voice: The
world's a hard place, and nobody helped me to get where I am.
By definition, the cynic's world can't be changed for the better,
because other people are weak, or lazy, or are themselves corrupt.
Cynicism is the opposite of accepting one's interdependence and
assuming one's responsibilities to society.

By now the reader may feel if not overwhelmed by responsibility,
then at least troubled by it. So much to be burdened by, so much
to do. With such weight on our shoulders, the bracing, exhilarating experience of being on our own, living without God and
religion, can easily give way to the urge to escape our obligations.
Is it any wonder that so many take consolation from religion,
giving God ultimate responsibility for literally everything?

But there is another dimension to this burden that can give
us back the exhilaration. It is an awareness of our own power.
Yes, our world was shaped before we got here, and yes, forces
beyond our control go a long way to making us who we are. But
a clear view of our place in various social spirals of responsibility also illuminates the role *we* play in them, which *we* can decide
to change. Seeing the extent to which we do indeed affect our
world frees us to consider ways, however small, we may change
it. I am talking about a shift from passive complicity to a spirit
of active participation. This may be done individually, but most
often it is done acting together with others.

French philosopher Francis Jeanson's difficult-to-translate
term for this is *citoyennisation.* "Citoyen" has a richer charge than
the English "citizen" due to its associations with the French Revolution, during which it became an accepted form of address.
Jeanson encourages breaking with the feeling of social helplessness imposed by today's globalization, and acting alongside

others to shape decisive areas of our collective existence. His term means "becoming citizens," or—because in doing so we must sharply reject what passes for "choice" and for "democracy" today—"militantly becoming citizens." In other words, actively assuming responsibility for our world can be an act of resistance to forces beyond our control.

When small groups of people in my town decided to go door to door to oppose the American war against Iraq, for example, they sought to talk with their neighbors about how the war affected their community. In the very act of doing so, something new is created. In reaching out to one's neighbors about "our" common problems, one shifts from being a private person to a public person. In such encounters one can feel oneself speaking in a different voice than usual, in public tones. In the process one often loses one's bashfulness by acting as a citizen, a social person. Any group of people doing this together becomes an active "we," challenging one public policy in the name of an alternative and better one. In the process, they do not simply think about what they should or might do, they do it, and live their social morality actively. In conversation among neighbors, whether in agreeing or debating, all those involved, for a brief moment, become citizens listening to each other and concerned collectively for their common fate. Such citizen activity involves experiencing our own interdependence with the rest of the world. It is self-empowering. And in breaking with our complicity, it has yet a further liberating effect: we are acting morally.

Expanding the narrow moral arc of the Ten Commandments into a genuine social morality underscores our belonging to the wider world and our obligations to it, as well as its obligations to us. Doing this means teaching our children accordingly. To get an idea of how this might look, it is worth comparing William Bennett's blockbuster *The Book of Virtues*, based on traditional individualistic and religious-based morality, with Colin Greer and Herbert Kohl's *A Call to Character*. Both books present stories and poems intended to help children become moral adults, and both books make responsibility a main theme. Bennett's stories are primarily selected to teach children to be responsible for themselves, with some slight admixture of military-style duty and loyalty and one or two bows to social responsibility. On the other hand, Greer and Kohl's much more expansive sense of responsibility places children in the wider world from the start, thinking for themselves, acting to convince adults to stop war, taking care of the environment, and seeing themselves as living among others who are very different but the same. Clearly, responsibility means two different things in the two books.

If we are responsible for so much outside of ourselves, because we are social beings, the converse is no less true: the society is responsible for us. Of course, today this means something sharply different than at any previous time in history. Slavery, serfdom, national oppression, class and racial oppression, war, and genocide have done their part to make human life, in Thomas Hobbes's centuries-old but memorable words, "solitary and poor, nasty, brutish, and short." No one who studies history or looks around the world today can ignore how fitting has been this description. Fitting, but not final. It has, after all, been made socially and politically wrong to discriminate against black people, to deprive them of political rights, to deny women the vote, to sexually harass them. Of course these evils still go on, but no longer with the force of law, and no longer as widely accepted social practice.

Again and again, oppressed human beings have refused to accept their oppression, and with allies have changed fundamental social relationships. In the process they have redefined what it means to be a human being. They have articulated new frameworks of rights a human being ought to have, and have made and won more and more concrete demands for universal rights and universal dignity. An African American child born toward the end of slavery in the United States might have been followed by generations of descendants who grew up under segregation, and by the 1960s their black children might have participated in the civil rights and black power movements. Today's African Americans are in some cases successful professionals, in others consigned to the urban underclass, but in most cases, the vast majority, living unspectacular, hardworking lives. Although they have been able to rise beyond its consequences to varying degrees, slavery has long since been abolished. And it is no longer politically, legally, or morally acceptable for whites to treat blacks as less than fully human.

However difficult the lives of many of them may still be, and however still touched by the traces of slavery and segregation, the current generation of African Americans face no statutory, and fewer informal and cultural, restrictions on their right to work, live, be educated, shop, eat in restaurants, move about physically, and travel. Of course, their lives, and U.S. society in general, remain poisoned by the society's unwillingness to act affirmatively to end racism and the heritage of slavery. But just as certainly, the half-empty cup is half-full of painfully won freedom, dignity, and opportunity.

It would be foolish to ignore the importance of the Ten Commandments in these lives. I mean not only the strength people have drawn from their religion, but also the determination to do right—to keep families together, to raise decent children, to earn a living, to be responsible workers. The importance of living morally and becoming models to one's family and fellow citizens cannot be overemphasized. But individual social morality does not stop there, but stretches all the way to, and nourishes, the

most noble vision humans have ever voiced, The Universal Declaration of Human Rights. Not very well known by Americans,
it was intended by Eleanor Roosevelt, the driving force behind
it, as an "international Magna Carta" for all people. Beginning
by proclaiming "recognition of the inherent dignity and of the
equal and inalienable rights of all members of the human family
is the foundation of freedom, justice and peace in the world,"
it stresses civil and political rights including the prohibition of
slavery and torture, the right to citizenship, property, equal protection under the law, democratic participation in government,
and freedom of religion. Since it was proclaimed in 1948, people
all over the world have further spelled out what it means to be
human—in thinking, writing, and teaching, in response to new
technical, political, and cultural possibilities, and most sharply
and dramatically, in political struggles.

The process of redefining what "we" are entitled to is always
a process of redefining who "we" are. Previously excluded and
subordinated groups have joined, and expanded, a previously
narrower discourse. Many who were at first voiceless, especially
colonial peoples in Africa and Asia, demanded entry, which
explains in part why the Universal Declaration of Human Rights
was followed, in 1966, by the International Covenants on Civil
and Political Rights and on Economic, Social, and Cultural
Rights. Both of these stress that "the ideal of free human beings
enjoying freedom from fear and want can only be achieved if
conditions are created whereby everyone may enjoy his economic, social, and cultural rights, as well as his civil and political
rights."

Obviously these are still only promises, broken as often as
honored. They reach considerably beyond the practice of any
particular contemporary nation-state, calling for higher education "to be made equally accessible to all," the right to work, the
right to "the highest standard of physical and mental health,"

the right to an adequate standard of living, and, despite the male pronoun, for equal rights for women, and equal pay for equal work.

Who is saying what to whom in this universal vision? One way to interpret its words and demands is to treat them skeptically, namely as the highest of generally acceptable human aspirations articulated by governments in 1948 and then 1966. "Generally acceptable" implies a series of relationships of power, yielding compromise between the various governments forming the United Nations, not only between the democratic capitalist societies and the then Soviet Union, but perhaps more significantly, between a handful of recently colonial countries and their former imperial rulers, and no less significantly, between still-imperial powers and their client states. The Universal Declaration and Covenants express what all of these could agree to say about human rights. They also reflect a compromise between the governments and their people about what might be regarded as the acceptable horizon of promises allowed to be promulgated in full view of the whole world. As such, the Declaration and Covenants reflect both a common denominator and an aspiration.

There is good reason to be cynical about these wish lists, promises by colonialist, racist, and despotic governments. Most of these governments were managing inequalities that they had no intention of dismantling. But rather than giving way to cynicism and dismissing these espoused rights as empty rhetoric, it is more correct to place these ideas historically. They could never have been put on a collective agenda of humanity three hundred, two hundred, or even a hundred years earlier. They began to be formulated during the Enlightenment, long before there was any collective institution to speak for humanity. But by the middle of the twentieth century, particular countries, and political and social movements almost everywhere, had evolved

to a point were such ideas were becoming widespread and politically compelling. Historical change had put on the agenda of
humankind "the advent of a world in which human beings shall
enjoy freedom of speech and belief and freedom from fear and
want." Something remarkable had occurred by 1948: rulers and
ruled together accepted the demands contained in the Declaration and Covenants as the norms by which they would agree to
have their societies be judged.

Despite all of their qualifications, cynics will not win this
argument. The articles of these documents embody the international consensus concerning human rights achieved by the late
twentieth century. They contain recent thinking about human
social morality. They explain how, without God, I can confidently talk about morality. They go so far as to assert that "the
individual, having duties to other individuals and to the community to which he belongs, is under a responsibility to strive for
the promotion and observance" of these rights. In other words,
they answer this chapter's opening question clearly: Yes, we are
indeed responsible for the plight of poor black Americans, and
for each other.

We are asked to work toward a time when every human
being achieves the kind of full human dignity allowed only to
the most privileged minorities in the past. No human being may
be deprived of this, and governments are to be evaluated on the
extent to which they achieve this. Accordingly, the Declaration
and Covenants deserve to be granted a moral force that reaches
well beyond the governments that agreed to them, because they
place a series of demands on the agenda that societies around
the world will continue to be judged by until they achieve them.
They are our promises to ourselves.

CHAPTER FOUR

Taking Responsibility for Ourselves

IN JULY 2007, THE UNITED STATES SUPREME COURT issued a decision in the case of Parents Involved in Community Schools v. Seattle School District No. 1, which effectively ended efforts to racially integrate public schools by assigning students to specific schools. Less than a year earlier, in November 2006, with black Detroiters voting nearly nine to one against, the voters of Michigan decisively approved an amendment to the state Constitution that outlawed any attempt to "grant preferential treatment in state hiring and university admissions to" any person "on the basis of race, sex, color, ethnicity, or national origin." Both the Supreme Court's decision and this "civil rights" amendment, similar to California's Proposition 209 passed ten years before, rejects the claim that our society has any responsibility to give special consideration to black citizens today. As Chief Justice John Roberts said, "The way to stop discrimination on the basis of race is to stop discriminating on the basis of race." The Constitution is to be considered "color-blind," and thus all individuals are considered to be on their own, equal before the law, and fully capable of determining their own fate.

What do these issues, so socially and politically controversial, have to do with my very different goal, namely developing a contemporary secularist worldview? If we sketch a map of what society's social and moral responsibilities look like if God is not in the picture, we can't go very far without noticing the other side of the coin, our responsibility to ourselves. It makes little sense to talk about our responsibilities in the world, for the fate of others, without understanding our own responsibility *for ourselves*.

This question is even more confused than the question of how far we are responsible for each other. As I mentioned, religious believers often hold individuals, being inescapably free and sinful by disposition, responsible for everything that goes wrong, and credit God for everything that goes right. Such explanations take the lazy way out. They avoid developing the intellectual and moral habits to intelligently negotiate our lives in today's world. They render us unable to concretely analyze specific situations, so as to sort through how global events are shaped by our own actions, those of others, social systems, and chance.

This is no less true of those whose popular religion frequently refers to "God's plan," or who turn to prayer automatically when facing the inexplicable, unacceptable, or uncontrollable. In America it has become a public reflex: A madman kills dozens of students in Virginia, and the president calls upon us to seek comfort in prayer; after an ex-employee's murder/suicide rampage at a Michigan accounting firm, the newspaper headline writer seems required to say that colleagues are praying for the two victims on the critical list although the article mentions this nowhere; the president sends soldiers to Iraq, and calls on their families and all Americans to pray for their safety. And those who are less religious speak constantly of fate, or of things that are "meant to happen," or of there being "a reason for everything."

Where is responsibility in all this? These religion-tinged responses show us that our culture does not encourage people to intelligently assume responsibility for their lives or demand us to explain the most important events and outcomes. We all seem confused. We see around us considerable distortion and little questioning about what is the actual balance of chance and individual choice in how things turn out, or the extent to which the social system intervenes in people's lives. Precisely what is within and what is beyond our individual control? Within or beyond our collective control? In Sunday school or public school we receive and we give little useful instruction in differentiating areas of individual or collective responsibility, or in distinguishing these from accidents or luck.

Whether we are religious or secular, in this society we often assume responsibility inappropriately, for example blaming ourselves individually for all that turns out poorly. Or we just as wrongheadedly take credit for things that benefit us whether or not we actually caused them to happen. As the joke goes about George W. Bush, there are those among us who were born on third base but think we've hit a triple.

Others of us are taught to blame the poor for their poverty. Do we, no less inappropriately, take credit for only what is pleasing to us, while assigning blame elsewhere for whatever is displeasing? It seems that many people assign credit and blame without paying much attention to the facts. How can we avoid ideologically and psychologically skewed, unthinking responses—and live our lives in such a way as to both take and ascribe responsibility clearly and appropriately, when and where it is due?

The task of assuming and ascribing responsibility creates a sharp divide between most religious believers and those who live without religion. Yet among secularists, some never think about such questions in a conscious, sustained way. Others see individual responsibility everywhere, while still others find social conditions at the root of all situations. Unless we find sensible paths for settling these issues, living a life that makes moral sense is well-nigh impossible. Our own long-term comfort as unbelievers, and thus in no small way the future of atheism, agnosticism, and secularism, depends on freeing ourselves from the confusion that surrounds questions of responsibility today. People trying to live coherent lives may find themselves tossing around in ambivalence, alternating dizzyingly between perspectives: now experiencing the overwhelming stress of feeling totally responsible, now feeling impotent before incomprehensible forces, and now being tempted to evade responsibility by depositing their concerns in the lap of higher powers such as fate, or chance, or God.

Are all individuals, as the anti–affirmative action activists argue, wholly capable of determining their own lives? Personal responsibility is a dominant theme among Americans, and not only because of the conservative ideological offensive of the past generation. We are brought up to believe from very early on that our fate is up to us *as individuals:* this, after all, is a cornerstone of the American Dream. Liberals may wish to help those who start off at a disadvantage, or to provide more of a social safety net, but they mostly have the same American Dream as conservatives. And there has been much reality to it: we are on our own here as nowhere else, and white Americans have always been less hindered by institutions, traditions, laws, and social policies than almost any other people. Our individualism is captured in the two symbolic experiences that have filled and energized this great country, frontier settlement and immigration. In the film based on the novel of the same name, *The Namesake*, about Indian immigrants, one of the main characters gushes, "In America you can do anything you want, become anything you want." Even today, this American sense of possibility continues to captivate and attract much of the world.

But how far are we actually free to make ourselves? What about all of the structures and pressures beyond our control that enter into what we are and what we do? Aren't many of us hobbled by debilities assigned to us by our class, race, or gender? If some of us receive poorer nutrition than others while growing up as a result of poverty or inadequate healthcare, how can we as adults be held just as responsible for where we wind up in life as those who are raised to be physically and mentally among the fittest? And aren't those of us growing up in a self-confident and highly literate culture, expected by family position and social environment, and still by gender, to succeed in life? Beyond family-transmitted personal skills, what about those who inherit wealth and position, those who are born on third base? Aren't these persons decisively advantaged over those lacking such tools and encouragement? To the extent that life is a race, or a series of ladders to climb, or whatever metaphor we want to use that points to universal competition, the educational system destines some of us to lose, others to win big, still others to wind up somewhere in between.

"Destined" is a harsh word because it suggests that some larger mechanism is at work, that there is little that we can do about the outcome. But what was already true at my high school is far truer today from one high school to the next. And this means in turn that claims of equal opportunity ring hollow, that stories about bootstraps are mostly myths. In short, for all our talk about

individual freedom, the results of the competition are largely
settled in advance. And in fact, don't most of us end up socially
and economically very near our starting point? If freedom means
having access to conditions essential for bettering ourselves,
huge numbers of Americans are not really free. If it means full
access to opportunity, a relatively small percentage are actually
free. But then how can we talk about responsibility for success
or failure where opportunity is unequal? Where black children
born in Detroit and white children born in Bloomfield Hills
have different destinies?

Many Americans, when confronted with such arguments, will
respond as if they've just read the early Sartre: In every situation
there is always a choice. Dismissing "determinism" and "excuses,"
they point to one or two cases of those born in poverty who have
overcome it and made good. After all, didn't Sartre himself say,
"Man is responsible for everything he does"? As he insists, correctly, we are much more than products of our circumstances
and environment; we are not raised like corn or cabbages to
yield a foreordained result. Our own spontaneity is absolutely
irreducible to any and all prior social or physical processes: "For
human reality, to exist is always to assume its being; that is, to
be responsible for it instead of receiving it from outside like a
stone." In the end, we make ourselves.

In everyday discussions, a political and social argument about,
say, inequality in education very suddenly becomes a philosophical argument over free will. Are the different kinds of freedom being mixed and muddled? Even in pronouncing his first
ideas about freedom, Sartre was aware that our power of self-
determination shares something with, but is not the same thing
as, political freedom—such as the right to vote, civil liberties,
freedom from discrimination, freedom of speech and assembly,
and freedom of movement. These political goals, aimed at for

example by the American civil rights movement and the struggle to end apartheid in South Africa, are different from but overlap with freedom of opportunity and other dimensions of social and economic freedom, such as the right to adequate health-care. Clarifying each of these dimensions, their overlap, and the differences between them, is crucial for all of us, believers and nonbelievers, because doing so is absolutely essential for making sense of what it means to be responsible for our fate in life.

What is free will? If it means that whatever I do is based on my own decision, what, for example, is entailed in deciding to lift an arm? Some cognitive scientists point out that by the time I have made such a decision, the neurological process of motion has already commenced. This seems to mean that free will is only an illusion—that all of my decisions and actions are determined by prior processes, of which I'm totally unaware. This becomes part of a larger argument: In a universe governed by physical, chemical, and biological processes, human beings, as physical, chemical, and biological beings, are no less determined than anything else by a chain of prior causes.

This assertion becomes less abstract if we consider it on the psychological level, where we sense that a host of processes is constantly taking place outside of our control or even our aware-ness. Some of these may stem from unresolved childhood trau-mas and conflicts, which continue to compel us to hurt ourselves or others. We may be responsible for ourselves, but the fact is that we often feel as if we can't help what we do. In today's world this, of course, is a reason that so many people seek out the help of psychotherapists.

Free will versus determinism: this is only one of today's per-plexities about freedom and responsibility that make it seem irresolvable. No wonder there has been a perennial philosophical

controversy over this issue. It seems as if the more we understand about human beings, the more *both* sides of the argument
become strengthened. We learn more about the historical,
social, and physical—and more recently the neurological—forces
behind our every thought and act, *and* we learn more about our
capacity—increasingly understood by thinkers influenced by
evolution—for reflective and deliberative decision-making. In
the words of philosopher Saul Smilansky, who has unflinchingly
probed both sides of the argument, there is a "fundamental dualism" between, on the one hand, our conviction that people are
free to choose and are responsible for their acts, and on the
other, knowing that their "identity and action flow from circumstances beyond their control." In trying to "accommodate
the deep insights of rival positions rather than simply dismiss
them," Smilansky boldly concludes that the debate is impossible
to resolve.

In fact, in the stress of twenty-first-century life, we confirm
the freedom/determinism dualism by holding tightly to *both*
sides of the argument. It seems as if we want to praise and blame
people for their actions and yet cannot restrain ourselves from
explaining these in terms of other, prior causes. This has been
strikingly evident since the attacks on the World Trade Center
and Pentagon of September 11, 2001. Shortly afterward, *New
York Times* columnist Edward Rothstein rejected the "injustice
theory" of terror as worse than nonsense: "Claims of 'root causes'
are distractions from the real work at hand," which is not to
explain why people felt motivated to act as they did, but to combat the terrorists. One of the most intelligent American senators,
Carl Levin, of Michigan, when questioned about the underlying
causes of terrorism at a forum commemorating September 11,
immediately bristled, summarily rejecting any such thinking as
showing sympathy for the terrorists. If the "root causes of terror"

are the terrorists themselves, the lines of responsibility are clear and our only task is to eliminate them.

This may help explain why the Bush administration ignored a 2003 event in New York, sponsored by the Norwegian government and attended by seventeen heads of state and three foreign ministers: "Fighting Terrorism for Humanity: A Conference on the Roots of Evil." The near-unanimous American response to 9/11 was rather to ignore any thinking about historical, social, and economic conditions in which U.S. policies might play a role, rejecting the tendency to see the terrorists' actions as explained by anything but the terrorists themselves and their evil religious ideology.

But if we glance at the master's thesis in town planning written by 9/11 hijacker Mohamed Atta at a German university, we cannot help asking, with journalist Hedrick Smith, why someone with such a bright future would destroy himself and murder others. Seriously looking for answers might lead us into his thesis itself, which explores agricultural communities in ancient Aleppo. It celebrates a past glory of Arabic civilization and shows the author's desire to use his talents for the greater good. But this is an opportunity absent from the lives of many young Egyptian professionals today. Before even asking about the content of his religion or Atta's psychological makeup, we might pause here to ask whether developing new skills in Germany would allow a young Egyptian to better participate in improving his own society. We cannot help thinking that perhaps the more educated he became the more frustrated Atta grew about his own stifled world, and about how slight were his chances of contributing to it.

Atta led one of the two groups that flew airplanes into the World Trade Center, and whether or not these speculations hold water, it should be clear that definite historical, economic,

political, cultural, and psychological conditions led to his decision to seek paradise and its blessed virgins. In reflecting on the
fact that he and his comrades hijacked an airplane and killed
themselves in order to murder thousands of innocent people in
the United States, how much weight should we give to these conditions? How much is due to deranged currents within contemporary Islam, which inspired the hijackings and recent suicide
bombings? What is causing these currents? And does exploring
all this diminish Atta's personal responsibility? Pondering what
led Atta to commit mass murder throws light on the dilemma
of understanding our own decisions. If we are all fully responsible for ourselves, what weight do we give to social conditions?
Or are we left between two terms of a seemingly irresolvable
dichotomy: individual decisions or social conditions?

When Zacarias Moussaoui was convicted of conspiring to
murder Americans in the September 11 plot, he was spared the
death sentence because a majority of the sentencing jurors concluded that "mitigating factors," that is, forces beyond his control, may well have influenced his participation in the 9/11 plot.
In the words of the jury, "the defendant's unstable early childhood and dysfunctional family resulted in his being placed in
orphanages and having a home life without structure and emotional and financial support, eventually resulting in his leaving
home due to his hostile relationship with his mother." Further,
his "father had a violent temper and physically and emotionally
abused his family." The reasoning must have been that Moussaoui's childhood experiences either diminished his capacity to
know right from wrong, or contributed to his hostility, or made
him susceptible to those whose plans for mass murder fit his own
need for revenge. The jury concluded that these experiences
limited his own responsibility for his actions, and accordingly
reduced his sentence. To some extent, they agreed, he couldn't
help himself.

While whites who self-identified as born-again or evangelicals—indeed, those most strongly attached to the Ten Commandments—voted 25% more heavily than other whites against affirmative action in Michigan, I have no doubt that many of them would nevertheless, like the Moussaoui sentencing jury, listen sympathetically to a defendant's story of how being brought up in insecure and abusive conditions led to committing a crime, and vote against conviction. Such examples show how people can ascribe responsibility fiercely, while at the same time acknowledging that "underlying causes" may lead people to act as they do. How do secularists avoid such inconsistency when thinking about ourselves, our own actions, and our fate?

These issues inevitably arise as we spell out what it means to live without God today. We are wrestling with the Sphinx's Riddle of the twenty-first century: What kind of being is it that is profoundly free, and yet whose decisions and actions are profoundly affected by forces beyond its control? As we try to answer this, we are swamped by other questions: Are we or are we not ultimately responsible for what we do? What is our relationship to what befalls us? What is our responsibility for how our lives turn out? Of course we have the absolutely indubitable sense of being the authors of our actions—and yet it is no less certain that many of our possibilities are given to us, that many of our thoughts and feelings, needs and desires, come unbidden. Is the correct answer that we are really responsible only for some of our actions? Or are we free and active agents, but only to a limited extent?

These are high-stakes questions. Because they affect how we live our lives, in one form or another they have bedeviled Western philosophers since the Stoics. They bear on how we stand in relation to everything that we do and everything we are. Answering them involves sorting out who and what causes various events and results, and requires decisive further moral, psychological, and even political steps. It entails deciding who deserves credit or who or what is to blame. All this may mean asking what needs to change so that things may turn out otherwise in the future. But it is above all a key question that atheists, agnostics, secularists, skeptics, and freethinkers have to answer for and about ourselves.

Early in the movie *The Grapes of Wrath*, based on John Steinbeck's novel, the ghostlike Oklahoma farmer Muley tells a flashback story of trying to stave off the bulldozer sent by the land company that took title to his farm when he defaulted on the mortgage. In the flashback, the young driver is preparing to knock down Muley's house and buildings. Muley aims his shotgun at the driver, who turns out to be a neighbor's son lucky enough to have found a job in this depressed region, and the young man tries to talk him out of pulling the trigger. If you shoot me, he says, the land company will only send out someone else. "Well, who *do* I shoot?" Muley asks. Desperate to keep from being dispossessed, he wants to know who is responsible. He changes his proposed target and then changes it again—from the young man to the bank to the Eastern land company. Each time the driver points out the futility of stopping what is about to happen. And then befuddled, unable to find a target that makes sense, Muley stands aside and watches as his home is flattened. As the flashback dissolves, it is clear that he never found out who to fire his shotgun at, and Muley, the living dead man, continues to haunt the remnants of a once-thriving community. Who or what was to blame? Perhaps it was not the capitalist system at all, but Muley's lack of farming skill, or his family's bad luck at getting a marginal piece of land, or the great dust storms?

Who *do* we blame? Americans are gripped by an autonomy myth that hides our various forms of dependency and rules out notions of freedom and responsibility that are not focused on the individual. Yet we only see half the picture if we understand ourselves this way, limited by the prevailing ideal of "detached" self-sufficiency. The American mythology of hardy and courageous frontier homesteaders does capture something important, but tells only a part of their story, skipping over their profound dependence on carefully developed national policies, virtually free land confiscated from Native Americans, and protection by the United States Army. Similarly, our no less heroic immigrant ancestors were prepared for by national policies, cushioned by networks of support, and were able to benefit from their new country's high standard of living and its hunger for workers. In making new lives, these people depended on a host of conditions absent elsewhere. Despite the myths, they were far from being completely on their own. For Americans to think fruitfully about freedom and responsibility today, then, means freeing ourselves from a distorted and radically individualist way of seeing our fate.

This is not easy to do. Autonomy is a myth that people happen to live by. The daily-life differences between the United States and most of the advanced European societies are significant and persistent: Americans are more accustomed to facing life's vicissitudes on their own than are citizens of any equally wealthy country. They seem unaware that there are alternatives. Still, some do manage to glimpse their interdependencies. At a deeper level of education or political awareness lies a consciousness of some of the conditions and institutions that make us who we are. So much so that in certain communities, notably among African Americans, the sharp awareness of oppression by outside forces and a sense of group solidarity enters into strong tension with stressing personal responsibility.

A few years ago, comedian Bill Cosby set off a storm by asking blacks to stop blaming racism for their problems. He lamented common cultural, sexual, linguistic, parenting, and behavioral patterns among the "lower economic people"—such as using the word "nigger" freely, profanity, poor grammar, giving children African-sounding names, children having sex, girls becoming pregnant, illiteracy, domestic violence. He urged them to take responsibility for their lives and families, to become educated and better themselves.

While cheered on by many in his audience, Cosby was also sharply criticized for elitism and for blaming the have-nots for their behavior under terrible living conditions. While the participants in the argument would have rejected the either/or of ignoring racism and terrible living conditions on the one hand or claiming that poor blacks bore no responsibility at all for their problems on the other, polarization occurred over where primary responsibility should be assigned. It is a generations-old debate: Are social and economic conditions and institutions most immediately responsible or is it the behavior of poor African Americans themselves? Are they trapped in living conditions requiring political action and a social movement leading to institutional change, or is taking personal responsibility the most urgent step?

The 2000-year unresolved history of philosophizing about such issues on a more abstract level suggests a general reason for our sometimes being convinced by the one side, sometimes by the other. Both sides are partially correct. The many compelling philosophical perspectives on freedom and responsibility reflect the fact that persons are made up of more than a single aspect. Much of the debate, and much of our confusion, follows from gaining insight into one of these dimensions and then going on to ignore or minimize the others. Intellectual historian Jerrold Seigel has made a major contribution to our self-understanding by discerning three essential dimensions in the arguments and writings about the self over the past three hundred years: the bodily, the relational, and the reflective.

As physical selves we are creatures driven by bodily needs and urges. As relational selves we are social and cultural beings. As reflective selves we become conscious of the world and our own existence—and contemplate our bodies and social relations, and even our own consciousness. My point is that we need to think these selves together.

As bodily selves, we obey all physical and chemical laws, are biological beings determined by forces beyond our control. We have our own individual constitutions: some of us are more energetic, others are more lethargic, or more passionate. On this level our selves, and our self-awareness, are directly physical and rooted in the needs of our body. Even as we labor and transform the world with our bodies, we must submit to the laws of both. As the various sciences make clear, we are a rigorously determined part of a rigorously determined universe. And, because we are bodies, we may be decisively harmed by a panoply of negative causes: inadequate nutrition, or early illnesses, or poor healthcare, or harsh environmental conditions. Or we may live in constant conflict between our physical needs and the possibilities for satisfying them. Or, if we are fortunate, no such problems may trouble us and we may mature in full strength and health.

Scientists are sometimes tempted to explain persons wholly from within this physical perspective. For example, recently a group of neuroscientists has proclaimed that "within the foreseeable future science will be able to both explain and predict thoughts and decisions, as well as sensations and emotions, based on observable physiochemical processes in the human brain." As philosopher Jürgen Habermas stresses in response, we disappear as persons if we give in to the temptation to take ourselves as no more than objects of explanation. What are the purposes of their observations, and what values do they attach to them? This conscious, acting subject, embedded in language, is the creator of norms and goals. She can never be completely reduced to an object of knowledge because she is the actor and knower, an intentional being. She is always behind every observation, every act of knowing. Habermas points to an inevitable dualism entailed in seeing ourselves from the outside and objectively on the one hand, and approaching our activities as intentional, rational participants who follow norms and give reasons for our actions on the other—as free subjects.

These subjects are social beings. With others, they develop collective identities, shared perspectives and values, using a specific language and following specific cultural styles. Yet in this second perspective, our selves are what our relations with society and with others shape us to be. We become persons only by growing up among other persons, members of particular societies and communities with all of their essential idioms and forms of expression, and as more or less advantaged participants in their hierarchies. It is largely as members of a social world that we receive our life possibilities—not only those possibilities that are strictly social, but also many of those related to our bodily needs insofar as these are experienced and satisfied in certain socially determined ways. Accordingly, our social belonging—to gender, class, ethnic group, race, or nation—can also be seen as strictly defining us, conditioning us to speak certain phrases with certain accents, giving us certain understandings, and habituating us to live according to certain other patterns and expectations. But at the same time our social belonging is also the terrain of our freedom, giving us our powers, including first of all our capacity of consciousness.

This third dimension of the self, the reflective, conscious self, is what we have in mind when speaking of being free to decide and to choose. It is on this level that our self becomes an active agent, the center of its own realization, directs its own actions, and creates order among its various attitudes and beliefs. Our sense of free will has its home here, and just as no human self is conceivable without language, so is it impossible to imagine persons without consciousness. In becoming self-conscious, we place ourselves at a distance from our own being, and as a result can examine, evaluate, and even change it. Here is where the self appears self-creating. Our attention to ourselves makes us the beings who perceive alternatives, who give reasons, who are able to remember—and thus to be—who they are.

So far I have been talking as if human beings had always existed as they are today, as if the terms I've been describing were not, each and every one, deeply historical. Yet it took millions of years for a human self to emerge with our ability to reflect. The capacity was not even present when fully evolved anatomically modern humans possessing brains the size of ours appeared and made cave paintings thirty thousand years ago. It is a product of our history. Even the characters of Homer's *Iliad*, so familiar in so many ways, and written down only about three thousand years ago, don't yet seem fully capable of giving reasons and being held morally responsible for their actions. Their gods, after all, are the ones who get them into and out of trouble, just as they are responsible for all cosmic and natural phenomena. Since Homer humans have identified more and more of the forces responsible for making the world as it is and our lives as they are. We have evolved socially and culturally in ways that make use of our evolved biological capacities to see where outside forces leave off and we begin. This historical process entailed no longer seeing supernatural forces all around us, separating supreme beings from daily occurrences. Then it required studying and acting on the world without referring at all to a god or gods. Over this long development, we have acquired whole new dimensions of our being, including explaining why we choose to act as we do.

Does this three-dimensional picture of the self, now cast historically, set us on the path to resolving our Sphinx's Riddle? Almost. It certainly begins to clear up some of our confusion if we see persons as at once bodily, social, and reflective, and thus in a sense both free and shaped by forces beyond their control. But something is still missing: a dimension of our being that we have developed the vocabulary and tools for understanding only relatively recently. Spilling into these three dimensions uninvited lies a distinctly different and fourth dimension: our unconscious self. This is our hidden self, seat of our dreams, source of unbidden urges and feelings, sometimes in conflict with what we know to be good for us. It often puzzles our conscious selves, to the point where we get used to asking why we act this way or that, often discovering motives and needs we were first unaware of. Regardless of the waxing and waning of Freud's reputation, we are all Freudians to this extent: an inward search can lead us to unconscious drives or desires that have been imposing themselves on us covertly but with compelling force until, or even long after, they are comprehended.

Does the notion of "mitigating factors" in criminal law introduce a note of relativism that, by explaining our behavior in terms of forces beyond our control, undermines our ability to make moral judgments? Not at all. It affirms that persons can and should be held to social norms of morality. When they transgress these, they should usually be seen as free and held fully responsible. But in some circumstances, the law acknowledges that people lack self-control and rationality, are driven by negative and destructive impulses of such force that they are less than fully responsible for their actions. When we come to this conclusion we do not ignore the norm-centered understanding of personhood, but conclude that to a certain extent the individual was incapable of the free and responsible action it entails. One's reflective and rational self—one's socially developed consciousness—is either not sufficiently strong, or has been overpowered by socially destructive desires.

But then how can any of us call ourselves free and responsible for ourselves when we are moved by unconscious needs and desires, when harmful external forces become internalized and motivate us without our knowledge? This is what happens, after all, when traumas caused by abusive parents, such as Moussaoui's father, or terrible living conditions, such as those suffered by many poor African Americans, come to dominate individuals. In other words, in principle consciousness may always be able to choose freely, but in reality we are often unconsciously compelled to act as we do by inner or external forces. In principle we may always be able to reflect, to weigh alternatives, and to give reasons for our decisions, but in practice we will sometimes discover that our stated motives were a smokescreen for unconscious needs that were actually impelling us. Even accepting the fact that humans have a highly evolved consciousness with a sense of responsibility built into it, circumstances beyond their control favor some people to develop this consciousness fully, others to have it become distorted or underdeveloped or constantly overwhelmed.

Asking about freedom and responsibility leads to a multidimensional self, but how does this clarify our understanding of how the self operates? As with Plato's account of the psyche in *The Republic*, are people sometimes ruled by one dimension, sometimes another, even though the dominion of reason is to be preferred? Do our freedom and responsibility peek in and out like the sun on a partly cloudy day? "More or less" or "sometimes"—are these the best answers we can give to the freedom and responsibility question?

Today's pervasiveness of advertising, especially in Western societies, points our way through the thicket. The enormous social wealth devoted to persuading people both commercially and politically might at first blush be showing how malleable humans are. After all, a great proportion of such advertising, including political appeals, is out-and-out manipulation. Its goal is to bypass conscious reflection almost entirely, often appealing instead to myths, fears, angers, and even infantile needs. Political media gurus confirm this by preparing "talking points," giving seminars, and writing about "words that work" and techniques of "framing" to put opponents on the defensive. In all this they quite scientifically and objectively focus on what people respond to, as if we were children.

Obviously they succeed enough to keep money pouring into a multibillion-dollar persuasion industry that has become vital both to the economy and the political world—but they do not control people. The pervasiveness of propaganda paradoxically testifies to the most important fact: consciousness will not be controlled, only persuaded. Evidence and reason, and the capacity of consciousness to critically evaluate truth, do matter. Yes, nearly all people can be manipulated some of the time (after 9/11, for example). Perhaps some people, alas, can be manipulated all of the time (more than one quarter of all Americans still believe that Saddam Hussein was personally involved in the attacks). But for all of its power over public opinion and domination of a submissive media, the Bush Administration could not forever hide the truth about Iraq and keep a majority of Americans supporting its war. Even if only eventually, truth will win out.

Advertising is, of course, a recent phenomenon. It is now so widespread for the simple reason that individuals are free to decide for themselves in historically new ways: where to live, where to work, where to take leisure, what to buy, whether to become partnered and whom to partner with, whether to stay partnered, whom to vote for, and even when to die. Humans are only now becoming responsible for themselves in all these ways, and many of the ways in which we remain unfree are also subject to historical change. Technological innovation, social evolution, and social struggles have created new zones of freedom and responsibility, and are likely to continue to do so. There is nothing final in the fact that both our freedom to choose and our capacity to reflect are seriously compromised in specific ways. And if vast numbers of individuals have a distorted sense of personal responsibility, this too may change over time.

But even the most driven and fearful individuals will make themselves. People, no matter how conditioned by external forces, no matter how unaware of the actual processes at work within them, no matter how passive they seem, are always responsible for their lives. What does this mean, Sartre's great insight, the heart of his philosophy? Sartre electrified and scandalized people everywhere immediately after World War II by claiming that humans are free and responsible for themselves in any and every situation. He famously asserted: "The slave in chains is free to break them" and "We were never so free as during the German Occupation." Despite their extravagance, Sartre wrote these startling lines only after carefully and patiently explaining the specific ways consciousness makes all humans free, all of the time—even the person being victimized by another's power.

This has a vital meaning in a world that has so many oppressions built into it, in which much of what we think, feel, and do escapes our control. As Sartre deepened his thinking to incorporate our social selves, he embarked on a great adventure of the human spirit, beginning with this core of freedom and then exploring the ways we are unfree by interrogating the social, economic, and psychic conditions under which we develop as persons, and the severe restrictions on this freedom. Integrating Marxism into his thought, he came to say: Yes, we do make ourselves—but the situation within which we do, and even the terms in which we do so, are imposed on us and remain beyond our control, in ways deriving from social structures and systems of power and privilege. Absorbing Freud, in works such as his biography of Gustave Flaubert, he went on to demonstrate precisely how one individual made himself not only from what his social belonging made him to be, but also from his family situation, including exactly how his most basic physical needs were met by his mother. Even in talking about mental illness, Sartre appreciated it as "the solution that the free organism invents in its total unity in order to be able to live in an unlivable situation." Neuroses, in other words, are our own, yes!, freely invented solutions to enormous stress.

But how is this different than the autonomy myth? Doesn't it amount to giving the individual a kind of absolute freedom, able to be exercised no matter what the circumstances? And has this always been so, or has it evolved historically? In thinking his way through these issues, Sartre came to qualify his argument without abandoning his starting point, winding up with a modest, but still decisive, margin of free activity. Freedom is "the small movement which makes of a totally conditioned being someone who does not render back completely what his conditioning has given him." Sartre elaborates on Frederick Engels' famous statement about men making their history in an environment that in turn conditions them: "But it is *the men* who make it and not the prior conditions. Otherwise men would be merely the vehicles of inhuman forces which through them would govern the social world."

Yet what remains of freedom in situations where we feel compelled to develop certain self-defeating behaviors for the sake of physical or psychic survival? This has been the lot of most of humanity during most of human history. People have been trained to hate their bodies, their sexuality, their thoughts and feelings that spilled beyond traditional gender roles. Children's personalities have been subjected to the injuries of class, race, and ethnicity. Homosexuals lived in conventional heterosexual marriages, women became irrational, conquered people became servile, colonial people learned their place, black men diminished themselves before whites. Each case entailed accepting someone else's definition as a way of being. What remains of free choice when the alternative is so dangerous it threatens one's very existence? It is difficult to hold ourselves responsible for who we are and what we do when many of our behaviors are dictated, when social and survival pressures to conform are overwhelming, and our capacities for reflection are stunted.

Although our freedom to choose at times is so shrunken that it is hard to talk about with a straight face, humans never simply receive the imprint of the forces acting on them. In making myself into what is expected of me, I am affected by demands, limitations, and threats, and these enter into my particular personality, habits, way of living my life, and goals. Whatever forces have shaped its components and imposed themselves on me, the resulting whole is mine, because I then make them into—me. I am not responsible for the materials I start with, or even my own skills, but it is me who makes something of them. I may, and often should, be angry at who or what gave me my starting points and who or what continues to limit my possibilities—but even so, it is me who constructs a life out of these. No one else, nothing else. In this limited but absolute sense I am responsible, as have been all humans before me, for the life and self I have made.

This attribution of responsibility holds true even for the neurotic whose greatest problem is an inability to take responsibility. Even if driven by unconscious motives, her actions and decisions belong to no one else. Psychotherapy aims one at owning these, becoming conscious of what one feels, clarifying one's conflicts, seeing why one acts this destructive way or that. The psychotherapist assumes the existence of a space of conscious reflection, however small, that can describe, observe, and evaluate these choices—the power to compare what we do with what we'd like to do, to recall the past, to discuss feelings. The psychotherapist acts as if there is always such a space to appeal to, offering the patient the possibility of seeing patterns, recalling their origin, and in the process taking responsibility for them. What I have done and how I feel may be beyond my conscious control, but in an essential sense they belong to me, are mine, and the therapeutic goal is to make them consciously mine and so reduce their power over me.

In a different way, the political organizer, trade union activist, or community organizer points out grievances and also asks people to see their patterns and sources of behavior, and offers the possibility of change. The forces to be understood and combated are social, often entailing real-world conflict. But before and even while engaging them, it is often necessary to overcome people's passivity and resignation. Accordingly, the organizer insists that there is no need to continue to feel hopeless or to see our situation as our fate, but rather that we can join together and become active participants in reshaping it. Reflection can lead to action.

Both types of interventions presume that we are not yet free, but that we are free to become free. They turn on our ability to see that we do indeed make ourselves and that we can change both the process and the results if we *take* responsibility. This means becoming fully conscious of what we have created or submitted to while we were only half-aware of it. This means shaking off the sense of being objects of our fate, and notic- ing, among other things, our own complicity in situations we may lament. This means deliberately and consciously assuming our place in a given spiral of responsibility. Taking responsibil- ity means overcoming the vague mood of helplessness, deciding to see ourselves as having created our lives. Of course doing so depends on conditions being propitious. It means asserting a will to consciously control future conditions as far as possible. It means accepting that we are free to become free.

So assuming responsibility for our lives does not mean that we exonerate all the forces beyond our control that have shaped our alternatives and limited our development. Just as we acknowl- edge what we have made of ourselves, our situation and capaci- ties, so we can hold other individuals, social structures, and institutions responsible for the conditions they have created for us. Sometimes this means giving credit, of course—and experi- encing gratitude. But it also entails a sharp awareness of the dis- abilities not only imposed on and built into people in the recent and distant past, but the limitations and distortions continuing to be structured into people at this very moment.

Gaining this awareness demands two things of us. The first is a complex understanding, one capable of integrating both a sense of responsibility and a sense of being subject to forces beyond our control. The second is a decision to take responsibility for our own actions and our roles. This leads to the determination to bring under our control as much of our world as possible. Yet it also demands acknowledging our unfreedom. Assigning responsibility for this means naming and combating habits, practices, values, ideologies, individuals, institutions, and forces that continue making us unfree.

Living without God, it turns out, not only entails taking the world on our shoulders, but also demands a self-confident determination to take responsibility for our own lives. Both tasks may appear as enormous burdens, but they belong to us only because they have become historically possible. Human life, and self-awareness, have evolved to the point where, today, it is becoming clear where we leave off and the world begins, as well as where the world leaves off and we begin. Our choice is no longer to take full and unlimited responsibility for areas of our life and to assign others to a supreme being, but to take and assign responsibility for ourselves and our world *as appropriate.* Living without God gives us such burdens only because they are our heritage, the product of human achievements—in fact, they are our privilege.

Once the world was alive with spirits and gods; rituals, sacrifices, and prayers sought to appease, satisfy, and cajole them. Early human consciousness ascribed much of what was most vital and vulnerable in life to immanent, superhuman powers that required constant attention to remain friendly and in our favor. Eventually such powers became simplified and placed beyond the sensible world. When people saw the world as ruled over by a transcendent God, they thought prayer and obedience would gain his good will. As anthropologist Marcel Gauchet describes it, seeing God as a distinct being having less to do with daily life, usually interpreted as religious progress, was in fact a decisive step toward going beyond religion. Gauchet reads the history of religion as a history of the waning and limiting of the religious consciousness as humans take greater and greater responsibility for themselves. Similar to Feuerbach and Marx, he describes the history of religion as the growth of secular consciousness—as a slow process of humans reappropriating from the natural and human world what they had once assigned to the deity.

Here, after all, is the deep link between living without God and becoming appropriately responsible for ourselves and our lives. As it emerges, then, secular consciousness simultaneously becomes aware of itself and its limits. The end product is humans animated by a clear sense of the various and multifaceted ways our world and our lives are within and beyond our individual and collective control. Living without God is only one side of a historical process in which we come to know ourselves and the forces in our lives, know whom and what to blame, and know when to claim and when to assign responsibility.

These thoughts bring us back to the starting point, the Michigan vote against affirmative action. We can now answer my opening question: Are black Americans fully responsible for their fate, as the Supreme Court has said and as a large majority of white people in California and Michigan have insisted? Yes, of course they are responsible, but at the same time the larger society is also responsible for righting past and present injustices and removing present obstacles to freely exercising that responsibility.

The obscenity of slavery was always that human beings—conscious, intelligent, self-directing, and responsible and free by their very nature—were forced to submit to being owned as property and subjected to the will of other human beings on pain of death. The obscenity of segregation was that by law, terror, and custom, it perpetuated second-class citizenship from birth to death. During the period of segregation, Northern blacks were freer and more mobile than in the South, but nevertheless were forced to live under racist conditions of school and housing segregation, massive employment discrimination, and socially accepted health and education discrepancies, as well as police harassment. These conditions have considerably moderated but not vanished.

In proclaiming themselves African Americans, black citizens have taken responsibility for their own identity while confirming their entitlement to full legal and political rights throughout the country. In just two generations an amazing number have fought their way out of poverty—reducing the nearly 90% poor of 1940 to about 30% today. To be sure, even among the black middle class, prosperity and status often seem fragile, especially because most lack the accumulated wealth and social networks of their white counterparts, and because of continuing discrimination. We are still generations from W. E. B. Dubois's "veil" being lifted.

Above all, one-third remain a class apart, impoverished, with few opportunities, pent up in terrible living conditions, preyed upon by the criminal class these conditions generate. They may get to interact with black police and public officials and see black sports stars and other black individuals on television as never before. But even though they now have equal citizenship, their hopes for their children are undermined by a stubborn culture of poverty, with its inadequate housing, terrible schools, restricted job opportunities, and absent fathers. Free to choose as never before, and free to move around as never before, young poor blacks are directly in charge of their lives as never before in America—but usually lack the means and the ability to do much more than perpetuate a self-defeating and violent youth culture that reflects their environment. Most of them are destined to move into adulthood producing and enduring disproportion-ately high rates of infant mortality, teen pregnancy, school drop-outs, adult illiteracy, un-employment, and disease.

Who or what is responsible? Black adults who have grown up in poverty are no less responsible for their own actions and lives than anyone else. Yet, like anyone else, the alternatives from which they choose come from elsewhere. Their family situation and physical surroundings are at one and the same time still affected by the heritage of slavery and segregation, a product of continuing social neglect and racism, and the socioeconomic result of being at the bottom of a lengthening ladder in one of the world's most unequal societies. And the skills with which young people learn to confront that environment are shaped by this history, and are skewed and limited by it. Most conscious beings who are free to choose, living in such conditions, cannot help but remain seriously underdeveloped, unable to magically invent themselves into the mainstream without appropriate skills, incentives, or opportunities. Free, they are thus unfree in decisive ways. They will become responsible for making their own lives, but they are certainly not responsible for the condi-tions under which they have to make themselves, or even for the skills with which they try to understand and adapt to their condi-tion. They are responsible for making themselves, yes, in a social situation that is responsible for their continuing deprivation.

Do they therefore have a valid claim for special consideration? Yes, they do. It should be obvious that once we understand our-selves as belonging to a society rather than being separate indi-viduals who happen to inhabit the same space, those who find themselves in inherited and socially sustained conditions of poverty *are produced by* these conditions. And these conditions are not their responsibility, but belong to all of us. Together we need to find a way of thinking and talking about this in order to make sense of it. And in doing so, we must again ask the question: Who will take responsibility for these conditions?

Why did nearly two-thirds of Michigan's and California's white voters reject affirmative action in the two referenda ten years apart? I am sure that some acknowledged the widespread existence of racism and inherited poverty, but believed that special consideration for all blacks was not the appropriate social remedy. Probably others believed the myth that since the poor make their own lives, they must also be responsible for their own poverty. Did any feel that blacks had achieved all the equality they were entitled to? Were some motivated by racism and fear of economic competition?

No one knows precisely why voters decide as they do, and exploring each of the issues surrounding affirmative action would distract us from answering the main question: What does it mean to take responsibility for ourselves? The demand of Michigan's Proposition 2, in the language of nondiscrimination and equal rights for all, turns out to have been spurious. One of the main buzzwords of its supporters was "fairness." Affirmative action was accused of being unfair—the idea was that African Americans have full citizenship rights and are protected by antidiscrimination legislation in a society that promises no more than this to any of its citizens. And that anyone demanding more is asking for "preferences." The implication, repeated again and again, was that most white Americans, living under the autonomy myth, believe that they are responsible for their own fate and no one else's, and so why shouldn't everyone else—black Americans especially—be just as responsible?

This is paradoxically confirmed in the Michigan referendum by the vote among those who, in at least one significant way, *do* acknowledge their dependency on larger social forces, namely labor union families. They actually voted by a slight majority for keeping affirmative action. Since union members include a disproportionately large number of black members, the more revealing exit polling statistic is that white nonunion families were significantly more likely to vote against affirmative action— approximately one-third more likely—than white union families. In contrast, as one polling result concerning the vote for Proposition 2 in Michigan shows, those who see themselves as most strongly connected to the Ten Commandments, namely evangelical white Christians, voted against affirmative action at an even higher rate than other whites. Apparently these are, of all Americans, least likely to be their brothers' keepers.

Among many poorer whites the notion of helping the disadvantaged black victims of past and even present oppression and discrimination must appear to be outrageously generous, given the fact that they have been raised to see every aspect of their own lives as their own responsibility. Their question is a powerful one: Why should they be asked to bear responsibility for the deprivation experienced by blacks when no one is proposing to take responsibility for their own deprivation? Why, it might be further asked, should it fall on them to pay the debt, through preferences given to African Americans in competition for jobs, rather than the entire society, through resources devoted, say, to nutrition, housing, education, or training?

Notice how our terrain has slowly shifted: answering the question about when and how far to take responsibility for ourselves as individuals leads back to the issue of how far we are responsible for others. Affirmative action is a murky solution to a dimly perceived and confusingly formulated problem. Accordingly, the debate has been narrow, perplexing, and mean-spirited. It has been about a distorted version of individual responsibility on the one side versus a distorted version of social responsibility on the other. On the contrary, if we could clarify both in a way that might generate a serious political will to help people help themselves, we would take a different direction: we would pursue a collective discussion about injustice on many levels, in order democratically to arrive at consensus about how then to proceed. But this requires thinking clearly about the vexing questions of our responsibilities—for our world, and for ourselves. The fact that all of us freely make ourselves should not blind us to the urgency of combating the forces that constrain us and limit our freedom.

CHAPTER FIVE

Choosing
to Know

ALMOST HALF OF AMERICANS REJECT EVOLUTION, AND
they do so not after close study and careful consideration, but
because of their religious faith. These believers, unlike liberal
Christians, most Jews, and the Catholic Church, still insist on
claiming that the book of Genesis is a literal account of the
origin of the universe, the earth, plants, animals, and humans.
They refuse to study evolution, or do so in order to refute it.
In so doing, they reject a decisive aspect of the world they live
in and a key part of its knowledge. Amazingly, in the country
that has long been among the world's most highly educated and
science-minded, where the importance of education is dinned
into everyone's heads morning, noon, and night, where more
than one in every four adults has graduated from college, these
citizens choose to be ignorant.

Creationism is not, to use Michael Shermer's apt phrase, the
only "weird belief" among Americans. By this he intends a belief
that people embrace despite an absence of scientific support. We

choose to accept them without, or even against, logic or evidence. Building on older definitions that link "weird" to forces beyond human control, including fate or destiny, the supernatural, the uncanny and the mysterious, Shermer applies it to beliefs that are bizarre or strange.

Alongside creationism, Americans are just as likely to believe in ghosts and UFOs, and only somewhat less likely to believe in witches and astrology. As a matter of fact, three-quarters of Americans admit to at least one paranormal belief, including clairvoyance (26%), ESP (41%), telepathy (31%), and communication with the dead (21%). Shermer includes Holocaust denial and racism among the weird beliefs he analyzes. Of course the term also fits almost all religious beliefs, but these do not seem strange or bizarre to many ears insofar as they are part of a Judeo-Christian paradigm that pervades American society. Furthermore, three key beliefs among these may not be at all weird in the strict sense, depending on how they are construed: the existence of God, of heaven, and of the soul after death. Such religious themes can be framed in a way that they stick to their own terrain, as Stephen Jay Gould argued, as matters of faith about which no knowledge is available, as long as they take care not to contradict scientific knowledge or logical reasoning.

Obviously, strange or bizarre beliefs are not confined to the margins. And yet except for creationism, they largely manage to thrive independently of mainstream institutions, to the point where popular demand draws media attention and exploitation, for example on television shows such as *Paranormal State*, *Ghost Hunters*, or the *X-Testers*. How is it that the vast majority of Americans choose to believe at least one paranormal belief despite our modernity, our stress on science, and the subjection of area after area of our society and our personal lives to rational analysis and organization? It may puzzle those of us who live by evidence-based critical approaches, but modernity and science do not keep people from embracing outlandish beliefs.

Nor does being educated or intelligent deter them. In some cases, such as ghosts and witchcraft, people may wholly embrace rationality and science in other aspects of their lives, while simply insisting that these particular beliefs have not yet been disproved. Or, as in the case of astrology, highly educated people may devote skill and energy to elaborating a system of explanation that seems to them as rational and scientific as any other. Often weird beliefs are linked to skepticism toward established truths and institutions. Holocaust deniers, for example, reject all evidence coming from eyewitnesses, mainstream historians, and government institutions, while perversely asserting their own cult of nonevidence.

"Embrace," "reject," and "choose" are all crucial terms in the discussion of such beliefs, and I employ them deliberately. To choose to know is to encounter the world in a specific way. It is a way of acting. It is to choose to reveal an aspect of the world, or to let it be revealed, or to accept what others with appropriate credentials, arguments, and evidence have revealed about it. The point is, as Jean-Paul Sartre said (in a little-known posthumously published book, *Truth and Existence*), to be ignorant is to choose to ignore; it is to look away from what there is to know. Creationists ignore, turn away from, refuse to acknowledge, what is there and waiting to be seen, and for which there is ample evidence: modern science's understanding of how the earth, plants, and animals came into existence. To choose not to know that humans have evolved over millions of years is to ignore what we have collectively learned is so. It is, in Sartrean terms, to engage in bad faith, an act of denial.

———

Was the Enlightenment overly optimistic in expressing confidence in ordinary people's ability to make sense of their lives and the world? This was once, after all, a radical claim about human capacities. Immanuel Kant proclaimed: "Dare to know! 'Have courage to use your own understanding!'—that is the motto of enlightenment." The Enlightenment, and the many-sided democratic transformations that have unfolded since, slowly produced a modern consensus; that all people can share in what John Dewey has called "the intellectual and moral resources which humanity has succeeded in getting together." For example, the first article of the Universal Declaration of Human Rights says that all people are "endowed with reason and conscience." Accordingly, later articles call for the right of freedom of thought and religion, and of opinion and expression. But are the claims warranted? Are all of us capable of all of this? Or do so many of us simply lack the capacity to share in humanity's collective intellectual and moral resources?

It has become a civilizational social, political, and intellectual starting point to affirm the general human capacity to develop reason, answer life's essential questions, live according to one's own lights, and become full and active citizens. But the proliferation of outlandish beliefs, and seemingly ineradicable prejudices based on half-truths, official lies, and media manipulation, are truly remarkable in a society awash in education and information, and where truth seems accessible at every turn. These facts of our daily life would make the Enlightenment weep.

How and why do they occur? Key arguments in this book have opposed various conventional wisdoms. One such conventional wisdom states that not all people have such a capacity for understanding. In other words, most or many are naturally stupid, or they are naturally lazy. Another claim is that there are no truths to get to, nothing beyond official stories on the one side and people's various individual and group stories on the other.

Everyone has their own truth. The first conventional wisdom is well-known as an old conservativism that has always rejected the Enlightenment on antidemocratic grounds; the second, asserted as postmodernist and proclaimed as democratic, portrays itself as a new radicalism that likewise rejects the Enlightenment. Both rest on persistent pessimisms, which are restated as soon as they are refuted, as is shown by the arguments on behalf of the "bell curve" and postmodernism. Accordingly, those of us who maintain both a sense of objective truth and a conviction about people's ability to arrive at it must face two urgent and challenging questions today, especially about Americans: Why, if people do possess the capacities to understand the world and themselves, do they so often choose not to employ these? And, given all the bizarre and distorted things people choose to believe, what does it take to exercise these abilities?

My favorite portrayal of people's ability to find their way past weird beliefs, prejudices, lies, misinformation, and distortions, is Sidney Lumet's great film, *Twelve Angry Men*. It tells the story of a jury reaching a verdict in a murder trial. Intense, angry, hard-edged, the film locks us into the jury room and, in a single ninety-minute scene, takes us through the tense struggle in which a lone holdout against conviction, played by Henry Fonda, resists the drive toward unanimity and slowly wins the support of one, now another, and now a third doubter. Bit by bit the prosecution's case against the defendant, an apparently Puerto Rican young man accused of killing his father, begins to crumble. As the facts are inspected more and more closely, one last man, played by Lee J. Cobb, still insists on the suspect's guilt. In a moment of high tension, he realizes that his rage against the defendant is actually about his own son, and dramatically throws in the towel.

In their attitudes toward the defendant, the prosecution, the witnesses, and each other, the jury members live out and overcome key obstacles to a reasoned conclusion. Almost all of them begin by accepting the government's case uncritically. They ignore any doubts and countervailing evidence. With great resistance, they overcome one after the other: misplaced respect, fear, racial prejudice, nativism, and class prejudice. These are held in place by bullying and ridicule, illogic and herd mentality. Each of these dissolves before our eyes as individual jurors choose to pay attention, doubt, make connections, reject their prejudices, listen to each other, and think their way through the holes in the prosecution's case, eventually deciding that it has not been proven beyond a reasonable doubt. Yet only after this taut and grim film ends do we realize how powerfully optimistic it has been. Ordinary people can make their way to the truth.

The film was released in April 1957, as the U.S. Supreme Court was considering whether to set aside the verdicts reached by such ordinary people in the Smith Act trials of over 100 members of the leadership of the Communist Party throughout the country. In these trials, juries were swept along by the Red Scare, uncritically embracing the official story without daring to demand that the government justify its contention: that participation in Communist organizations, including reading, believing, and teaching Marxist texts, without any preparation for revolution or violence, was sufficient to convict these people of being part of a conspiracy to "advocate, abet, advise or teach the duty, necessity, desirability or propriety of overthrowing the Government of the United States [by] . . . force or violence." The fact that these Communists were tried for their ideas, as opposed to their actions, is demonstrated in the prosecutor's reflection in the film account of one of these trials, *First Amendment on Trial: The Case of the Detroit Six*:

> We used to read the inflammatory passages to the jury. . . . Our theory was they were using them as a guide to action. You know, there was something eerie about the whole thing . . . those

books were in all the libraries, whether you agree with them or not, and that, you know, that was the basis of the government's evidence—all of these books.

In mid-June of 1957, the Supreme Court ruled that it was no longer acceptable to imprison people for their ideas, without actual evidence of insurrectionary action. Of course the juries had been constrained by the law to construe illegal activity quite liberally, but in retrospect, it is also clear that until that moment, every Smith Act trial jury uncritically went along with a systematic government campaign to destroy the Communist Party, stifle dissent, and inhibit free speech. Leadership in the Communist Party was enough to ensure conviction.

Fifty years later, this true story is a chastening counterweight to Lumet and writer Reginald Rose's hopeful fictional picture in *Twelve Angry Men*. People can, but do not necessarily, demonstrate the patience and attention, rationality and skepticism, freedom and sheer energy, needed to arrive at a conclusion on their own, beyond a reasonable doubt, that gets to the truth of the matter. And they seem especially susceptible to going along with the official story, to believing just what their public officials are trying to get them to accept. As many of those supporting President Bush's campaign of half-truths and unfounded allegations against Saddam Hussein in fall and winter of 2002–03 slowly learned, at enormous and continuing cost to Iraq and the United States, democratically elected governments can successfully twist and distort and lie, and the opposition party, the media, and ordinary citizens can choose to go along.

Twelve Angry Men and *First Amendment on Trial* show only a few of the impediments that keep people from employing the capacities prized by the Enlightenment and presupposed in the Universal Declaration of Human Rights. As the proliferation of bizarre beliefs shows, even when people free themselves from official stories they do not necessarily choose to enlighten themselves. Paradoxically, although knowledge is everywhere, the will to know is often absent, or goes haywire. We have seen one fictional case where people manage to generate the will, and collectively find their way to its accompanying skills. But we live amidst countless real-life situations where people devote great intelligence to weird beliefs, let themselves be manipulated, ignore vital truths, or just go along in ignorance.

A lifetime of teaching has convinced me that nothing so simple and straightforward as more information or education can be counted on to generate the will to know, eliminate the desire to believe outlandish things, fortify people against being manipulated and lied to, and equip them to think for themselves. Contrary to the optimism of many Enlightenment-influenced secularists, ignorance thrives among us despite the massive cultural emphasis on knowledge and schooling.

Americans are among the most highly educated people on earth, yet in over thirty other countries, including every other developed society, a higher percentage of the population accepts evolution. And by huge numbers: in most of these the difference is fifty percent greater. This discrepancy is not due to the prevalence of religious belief, as we can see by considering that in Ireland, with as high a rate of belief as the United States, 60% more of the population accepts evolution.

American college graduates, for example, are no less likely than anyone else to believe in UFOs or witches; one in three continue to believe in ghosts, one in six in astrology. Although half of graduates and postgraduates acknowledge that "Darwin's theory of evolution [is] proved by fossil evidence," the other half disagree with this statement. These numbers, troubling enough to those who place their hopes for general enlightenment in colleges and universities, are positively consoling next to the puzzling fact that only about one-third of U.S. college graduates (31%) and postgraduates (35%) admit to believing in evolution—while about 60% accept creationism. And next to the fact that outside of the U.S. other strange beliefs such as in witches, ghosts, and astrology, remain widespread. In Britain, for example, astrology has replaced religion as the number one set of beliefs.

What is it that encourages people to wish to know what there is to know, and to be able to recognize it? To return to the old antidemocratic conservatism, perhaps the will to truth is rare? Paradoxically enough, in one of the few instances in his works where ability or its lack is actually demonstrated, Plato, the father of all such conservatisms, has a slave boy comprehend the Pythagorean theorem. And in *The Republic* he lays far more stress on upbringing and social environment than on innate abilities. He speaks of the folly of supposing that education entails putting knowledge into a psyche that lacks it. Rather, he emphasizes, the goal is to encourage a process more akin to conversion, to find ways to dispose future rulers to value knowing. His entire educational system is focused not on creating brilliant or even intelligent people, but on placing future rulers in the kind of harmonious and salubrious environment that nurture their desire and capacity to distinguish between truth and falsehood.

Dewey, differing enormously from Plato in both political orientation and philosophy, nevertheless understands the central task in similar terms. They both make the will to know decisive, and seek to nurture it. They worry most of all about generating the environment, values, and habits of mind that allow the will to know to ripen into a positive human power.

Whether teaching working adults or traditional eighteen-to twenty-two-year-olds, encouraging the will to know is the

master task of the classroom. Success turns out to be rare
because obstacles are everywhere and enormous. Ironically college teachers, like other teachers, quickly get quite used to a fact
that, on the face of it, is quite preposterous: most of one's time
is not spent teaching and learning, but coping with, and trying
to overcome, the many institutional, social, political, cultural,
economic, and personal barriers to doing so. During a large part
of my own career as an educator it was my privilege to teach
adult students in the open-admissions interdisciplinary studies
program of Detroit's Wayne State University. From our experience together I have learned an immense amount both about the
obstacles keeping people from choosing to know, and the drive
that sometimes lifts adult students over those obstacles.

What are the obstacles? First, it is worth remembering that
they, too, are responsible for their choices, and yet, like everyone
else, their alternatives and even their own tools have been given
to them by forces beyond their control. *Twelve Angry Men* and
First Amendment on Trial show a few of the constraints we all share.
Among the others, the one most talked about has to do with the
pressures of the consumer culture and the media. These generate
a widespread sense of impatience and distraction, in addition to
their enormous hidden power to manipulate the ways people
think. This is reflected in the outrageous fact that 30% of Americans continued to believe that Saddam Hussein was involved in
the 9/11 attacks long after this was disproved, one of the most
fateful weird beliefs of the early twenty-first century.

No less important are the constraints imposed by social class.
It is simply true: those toward the bottom of the social ladder are
generally most prone to hold the kinds of weird beliefs I have
been talking about. This is because they develop and exercise
their powers of insight and intellect under the most unfavorable

conditions. Sometimes it seems as if the entire culture and society conspire against allowing them to see clearly.

A typical student was a black single parent, age forty, who worked for Blue Cross and attended class one or two nights a week. She would come to class directly from work, having called home to make sure the children had eaten and done their homework, picking up some fast food on the way and eating it while driving. From time to time her supervisor would have her stay late and she'd come into class after the in-class writing assignment was over. Their lives filled with stress and distractions, working adult learners struggle in ways unimaginable to more privileged young students, especially those who have been given the opportunity to go away to school and immerse themselves in college life.

Indeed, the meaning of "going to college" has changed significantly since the massive expansion of higher education in the last third of the twentieth century. Despite the huge numbers of people participating in tertiary education in advanced societies like the United States, social class matters not only in terms of who is able to pursue it, but no less important, in terms of what kind of higher education they are able to receive. A complex system of tracking and expectations sorts students into a hierarchy of paths, and then filters them into different grades of education, the lowest being job training and part-time college taught by part-time faculty and with no campus life. Such simple experiences as having time to reflect free from the business of life, and having opportunity to interact with other students in a leisurely way, are rare for almost all working-class students, even rarer for adults with family responsibilities who work full-time.

Nevertheless, my typical student hung in despite family, work, time, and financial stresses and thoroughly enjoyed the considerable classroom time a one-night-a-week, three-and-a-half-hour class was able to devote to open-ended discussion and small-group interaction. Moreover, she had high levels of self-discipline and enough motivation to come to class ready to participate. Does this mean she had greater desire to learn than younger students? No and yes. Her world view was already largely formed, and she was unlikely to be asking about the meaning of life or which life directions might best appeal to her. But she certainly was highly motivated, took in what she learned, and began to formulate specific learning goals—in this sense she became an "intentional learner." And she took seriously what she learned—about history, about literature, about philosophy, about science, about society.

One internal obstacle began to surface during this process. Her religion, at the center of her sense of community and identity, and an anchor of her life, began to conflict with her growing understanding of science and of how to ascertain truth. My sense was that she began to feel that fully embracing the available intellectual resources—science, rationality, debate, and discussion—meant abandoning her moral resources. And so, for the deepest of reasons, she held on to both: her commitment to learning and her commitment to religious truth. She absolutely refused to compromise on wanting the best possible science education for her children, and absolutely refused to consider nonliteral ways of understanding the book of Genesis that contradicted her pastor's stress on its perfect truth.

In chapter one I mentioned the conjunction Pippa Norris and Ronald Inglehart found between American inequality, individualism, scantiness of social provisioning, and our enormous religiosity. Their point was that people whose lives are insecure will feel a greater need to seek religious explanation and solace, and the specific statistics correlating religious belief to income bear this out. But much more is at stake in African American religion, involving not only consolation but a sense of peoplehood, moral strength, dignity, social equality, and tolerance. These values nourish what Michael Eric Dyson and Cornel West, the one an ordained Baptist minister and the other a professor of religion, call its "prophetic" features. Paradoxically, this makes it possible for African Americans to accept many fundamentalist beliefs, including creationism, while at the same time remaining resistant to the autonomy myth that blinds much of American society. Certain situations can thus simultaneously generate both the will to ignore *and* the will to truth.

In any case, the interdisciplinary studies program no longer exists, and my typical student of the past will no longer be attending Wayne State University, unless she can negotiate the remaining pathway, geared to younger students, and do so without advisers, faculty, and admissions procedures geared to her situation. But in this and other state universities, how well do those pathways function in providing students the opportunity to develop the will to know? Two distressing trends preoccupy many educators today: the enormous and rapidly increasing amount of available and essential knowledge explaining an increasingly complex world, and the distressing fact that even well-educated people often don't develop the skills needed to cope with it.

A single day in any life today demands that we learn constantly about both the basics and the latest knowledge concerning health, politics, household management, and many other broad areas. It requires plowing through enormous quantities of information and necessitates making constant decisions about what is relevant and not, and, when one has learned enough about a topic, how to integrate new information into what one already knows, and how to apply it.

How and where do we become equipped to make sense of the world? Today people are dependent on schools to furnish them with the ability and knowledge needed to function. We have to constantly learn and revise—whether about infant care, physical and mental fitness, nutrition, and a hundred other vital areas. No wonder higher education is widely regarded as *the* path to becoming fully functional. And it is increasingly clear that not just any higher education will do. Life today demands that we become active, intentional, and adaptive learners of new ideas and information rather than passive absorbers of a relatively stable body of knowledge. And these very habits or abilities, always mentioned among the key aims of contemporary liberal education, are precisely those required to be able to live without God. Among other advantages, people who manage to develop such habits and skills will be less susceptible to believing weird things. They will be more likely to sense their connectedness with the rest of the universe, nature, history, and the global society, and will be more disposed to understand both the centrality and limits of their own responsibility, for the rest of the world and themselves.

How well is the American education system currently doing in producing people with such habits and skills? By their own testimony, graduating seniors tend to be enthusiastic about their growth, especially in understanding people of other backgrounds. However, the little objective evidence that has been gathered is not encouraging, indicating that only 6% are "proficient" in critical thinking and 77% are "not proficient." And do they go beyond passive learning and trying to remember what they are reading and hearing, to active learning in which they learn to question, validate, and apply it?

To receive a "general education" at my own university a student must negotiate a menu of over 250 courses from which she selects, detailing no less than nineteen essential skill, content, and exposure areas. The highly selective University of Michigan has developed a less unwieldy structure and a more relaxed goal: instilling understanding and appreciation of at least some specific major areas of knowledge. But many of its students have access to small "learning communities," in which they become active learners, learn to work with others, and study in ways that can be interdisciplinary and integrative. Still, no program at either university seeks to teach all students the interrelatedness between the various pieces of knowledge learned in their vast intellectual cafeterias. Michigan State University, on the other hand, tries as well as it can to develop the skill of making sense of the whole in its centers for "integrative studies" in the arts and humanities, general sciences, and social sciences. This is a more focused and serious effort, backed by significant, if limited, resources, to overcome the fragmentation of learning built into most higher education today. Even so, its great promise exists in serious tension with other functions of the modern research university: students want to get these courses out of the way and senior faculty aren't eager to teach them; faculty are not accustomed to teaching in genuinely interdisciplinary, integrative ways; and the classes are too large to allow for active learning.

For the most part, active learning takes place during graduate education. And, despite its narrowed focus, here is where the sharpest dropoff in weird beliefs can be seen—over 50% fewer among those who have completed a graduate degree than among those who have achieved a bachelor's degree. Graduate students become intentional learners by setting their own goals, and they engage in active research, no longer simply receiving and recalling knowledge, but now applying and creating it. Graduate education trains people pursuing it in ways that change them: an active researcher who knows what it is to know will have significantly less tolerance for believing in UFOs, witches, astrology, or the devil (although apparently more accept reincarnation!).

Still, at the completion of an undergraduate education many Americans feel that they have gained a great deal. They wind up with an entry-level job qualification and considerable experience in the world of knowledge, having taken thirty to forty separate classes. They gain a wide exposure to several areas of knowledge, take several courses in a specific major field, and learn a number of specific skills. Certain kinds of social, personal, and educational empowerment result from a college education, but it is fair to say that many graduates will have received scanty experience in the habits and skills that lead people to know how to pose life's important questions and begin to answer them.

Belonging to an impatient culture promising instant answers, often poorly equipped and overwhelmed, people manage to piece together their fragments of faith and knowledge, including their education and religious upbringing, as best they can. Some of the most curious people restlessly surf the Internet in hot pursuit of questions that their schooling has not helped them even to ask, let alone answer. They often begin by being rightly suspicious of all official stories and seeking more compelling explanations. In the infinite space of the Internet, with the whole culture at one's fingertips, millions of answers cry out. It is the freest of all free markets, yet people are rarely trained to negotiate it.

With immense energy people search their way among gurus, conspiracy theories, spectacular shortcuts, easy answers, the latest political scandal, parodies of ancient wisdom, pseudo-scholarship decked out in scientific trappings, real knowledge and thoughtful reflections, newfangled or eclipsed religious and political wisdom, every established and every insurgent point of view, and sheer nonsense—and they are free to consume it and reassemble it as they wish. People pick and choose among these and often embrace bizarre beliefs, Shermer concludes, for four reasons: they "make us feel better," they tend to "offer immediate gratification," they promise "a meaningful and satisfying system of morality and meaning," and they give us hope. What kind of outlook does this lead to?

The most common and least recognizably weird of weird beliefs is: "Everything happens for a reason." We hear the phrase at every turn in the United States today: spouses telling why they met each other or why they broke up, one baseball player explaining why he didn't make the team, another explaining why he made the team, or anyone reflecting on a coincidence—a student softening the blow of a failing grade, a cancer patient coming to grips with her illness. Good happenings or bad, personal tragedies, disasters, matters of chance, striking coincidences, enormous disappointments, the unexpected—all become rationalized as being part of a larger plan.

The maxim mixes events that have comprehensible causes beyond our control, or that we produce from our own actions, with things that are pure accidents. All become the mush of a totally deterministic universe in which every last thing has a meaningful cause (but no one knows what it is) or is planned by a superhuman mind, presumably directing things for the best (and whose logic is also unknowable). Our map of interdependence is erased, with all of its specific detail, supplanted by a vague and unrecognizable force or will. One's responsibility for oneself and the world dissolves into this. And those who may be held culpable, individuals and institutions, are spared any reproach for whatever goes wrong. As this low-grade sense of fate or God or whatever percolates below the surface of American life today, many of us who lack a sense of control over our lives fall back on it, as do many traditionally religious people—and so do many others.

And it cannot be completely dismissed. "Everything happens for a reason" claims, vaguely, that what we experience, but whose reasons we can't comprehend, is part of a larger pattern—which is often true. It expresses people's hunch, often quite wise, that what happens is linked to larger forces and causes than those we have been trained to grasp. And it is often a wish to see justice done, even if only ultimately, and a hope for real meaning where there seems to be sheer randomness. But the event winds up buried in a half-baked sense of destiny. Life's disappointments and absurdities, its systematic evils and unspeakable barbarities, all become less disturbing, accidents are banished, an overall order is proclaimed to govern us, and bad things only happen for a larger good. Everything, after all, is meant to happen.

But this casts things in a way that usually ends discussion rather than beginning it. A healthy sense of linkages, larger purposes, and logics and forces beyond our control might lead someone to an environmental, epidemiological, sociological, political, economic, and historical study, and yield important insight. What if we work at making this vague intuition concrete rather than recirculating empty profundities? We can often get somewhere—as long as we are willing to admit that things may be happening randomly, or for no reason at all, or for dozens of reasons. We can connect the dots if we see a discernible pattern, and we have to learn how to shrug our shoulders when they don't. Yes, much of life happens because we ourselves have brought it about, and if we take responsibility for this and bring it into the light of day rather than assigning it to forces beyond our control, we can begin to understand our fate a little better. But also, much of life happens by chance, is inherently beyond anyone's control, and if we strengthen our ability to tell when this is happening and when it is not, we'll be better able to know when to submit and when to resist. Making sense depends on knowing when to deploy the one approach and when to give up and use the other.

Disasters especially strain our explanatory powers, and expose their weaknesses. They demand that we make sense of what is happening and why, but this means being able to accommodate several dimensions of an event at one and the same time—the natural, the long-term social, the immediate political, the individual, the random, and the unknowable. And they demand sorting out myth from fact.

When Hurricane Katrina and its aftermath destroyed much of New Orleans, efforts to understand in these various ways were strikingly evident, as were efforts to obfuscate. Michael Eric Dyson's *Come Hell or High Water* tries to make sense of the disaster and to assign responsibility appropriately—what part to nature, to specific individuals, to institutions, to ideology, to social and political policies. Most of the book reads as an indictment of the Bush administration's hostility to an active government, its cronyism in appointing incompetents to important posts, its inability to take decisive action to help people, its indifference to black suffering, and its eagerness to pass the buck for its fumbling. Dyson criticizes the federal government for its desire to turn the key task of reconstruction over to a for-profit mechanism that seems destined to destroy the character of New Orleans and exclude its poorer residents. Above all, he takes on all those who blamed the victims for their lack of urgency and planning and for their dependence on the government, and he criticizes the media for sensationalizing the few cases of those who broke into stores, usually for food.

Although focusing mostly on government failures from the moment the storm was predicted and not saying much about the vagaries of nature, Dyson also discusses longer-term issues: generations of environmental destruction that intensified Katrina's effect, persistent societal complaisance about black poverty, lack of concern for the precariousness of the geographical situation of New Orleans, engineering failures, and political diversion of funding. Only after developing his many-sided explanation does Dyson turn to what for an amazingly wide spectrum of victims and observers was their first response to the disaster: Where was God when Katrina hit? "Could it be that God caused Katrina?"

In a discussion of religious responses to Katrina, Dyson criticizes those who avoided any real attempt at explanation—both those who sermonized about God punishing New Orleans for its sinful ways and those who blamed the homeless victims for their poverty. In making God responsible for literally everything that happens on earth, and on searching for his intention to reward or punish us at every moment, all such explanations qualify as weird. But one aspect of Dyson's own call for a "prophetic" religious response undermines his effort to make sense of the disaster and its effects. After highly detailed chapters of narrative and analysis and in the midst of a sophisticated discussion of theodicy Dyson says, almost as an aside, that it is absurd to ask "what we did wrong" to provoke such a punishment. He says that "God's grace spared the survivors." Then he goes on to narrow his claim: "Although God's grace may account for why some poor folk lived . . . it appears that class position and skin color kept others from facing the fury of the storm."

This is the only place in the discussion where Dyson's religious faith takes over from, and contradicts, his skills as a social analyst. Admitting that we simply don't know why some survived and some didn't, or accepting luck or chance, would mean something rather different: In trying to understand events and lives, we sometimes have to shrug our shoulders. Instead, Dyson momentarily averts his eyes from the earth and, without concern for evidence or logic, turns them upward, choosing without explanation to search beyond humans and nature to explain what happened. His prodigious effort to make sense of the Katrina disaster to this point leaves us asking him, just as he asks the conservative ministers he criticizes: Why now turn to God, when the situation, like so many in our lives, demands pursuing its own logic as far as we can go, followed by the humility to admit ignorance when the trail runs out?

Certainly Dyson's outlook is more humane than that of vindictive fundamentalists. But is it any less strange that Dyson turns to God out of love for people who are suffering and because of a lack of other explanations, rather than invoking God in blaming them? While it does matter that, until that moment, Dyson's efforts support the idea that despite all the obstacles, we can make sense of our lives and our world, continuing to make sense of things that matter also depends on shunning this "God of the gaps" that Dyson, like many people, deploys when he has no other explanation.

This chapter began with two premises—that there is such a thing as objective truth, and that people are capable of arriving at it. I posed two questions, the first about why people often don't exercise this capacity, and the second about what it takes to do so. It is time to revisit the premises to see whether they still make sense. It turns out that both need to be qualified. Yes, people are able to find solid bearings based on real knowledge, but only if they choose to do so. And yes, knowing the truth is possible, but only if we humbly accept how contingent and fallible—and subject to constant revision—that truth is likely to be.

In *Truth and Existence*, Sartre distinguishes between the decision to ignore reality and the decision to reveal it. He is helped by the two meanings of the French *ignorer*: to not know, and to ignore. In English we preserve this connection between the act of not noticing something and the state of lacking knowledge: in the shift from *ignore, not paying attention* to *ignorant, the condition of not knowing*. Although this book is the only place where Sartre explicitly presents anything approaching a theory of knowledge, it is suffused with his existentialist sense of freedom and choice. This means that he makes the act of knowing into an act of will, a free decision—and a moral issue.

To choose not to know is to engage in bad faith. In ignoring, we seek to deny what we in some sense already know is there, and we degrade ourselves by willfully suppressing our awareness of it. This is because we don't want the situation we are ignoring to be the way it is: through ignorance we seek a kind of fantasy makeover of the world so that it fits our desires, rather than adapting ourselves to it by knowing it as it is and acting accordingly. We reject a situation that may be troubling or disheartening, threatening or terrifying. Sartre says: The "will to ignore is . . . the refusal to be free."

With the example of creationism in mind, we can appreciate that there may be many reasons why someone would choose to ignore evolution, or turn away from it, or deny it. Whether or not people accept evolution or reject it is often conditioned by forces well beyond their immediate control—being raised in a subculture that believes in absolute knowledge based on faith and authority, being trained in the schizophrenic attitude of rejecting science while living by its fruits, schooling in biblical interpretation that insists on accepting the literal truth of chosen passages of the Bible, obedience to parents and fundamentalist religious authorities who anathematize evolution, being part of a community that stipulates belief in creationism as a requirement of belonging. In addition, like everyone else in American society, creationists are subject to a culture that often fails to equip people to think scientifically, to conflicting mountains of knowledge demanding to be assimilated daily, and to schooling that does not insist that people develop and exercise their capacities to know actively and integratively. Nevertheless, even if we might explain in these various ways some of the forces that make creationists fearful of using their reason, the fact remains: embracing creationism is a refusal of the responsibility, as Sartre calls it, to "act, create, reveal, verify, accept." To do so would lead to reconciling one's faith with the realities of life rather than vice versa. Rejecting evolution is a choice to be ignorant.

On the other hand, the choice to know, to reveal, to use reason actively, to synthesize what one knows, is also the decision to give up any pretense to absolute knowledge. It is a statement of humility. It entails allowing oneself to enter into discussion, to submit what one says to the judgment of others, to be proven wrong by them, to be seen as fallible, and thus to realize that any particular piece of knowledge is always tentative, always subject to revision, always demanding verification. This in turn implies a commitment to a communicative process in which we are always in dialogue with others, and in which they are always looking over our shoulders and commenting on what we claim to be true.

It also means that we are capable of far more than "just survival and reproduction and comfort" and in fact have a unique privilege among creatures: that of learning and understanding. In *Why Truth Matters* Ophelia Benson and Jeremy Stangroom state this beautifully:

> [R]eal enquiry presupposes that truth matters. That it is true
> that there is a truth of the matter we're investigating, even if it

turns out that we can't find it. Maybe the next generation can, or two or three or ten after that, or maybe just someone more skilled than we are. But we have to think there is something to find in order for enquiry to be genuine enquiry and not just an arbitrary game that doesn't go anywhere.

Truth shifts historically and is framed according to one's disciplinary standpoint. It is never absolute but is objective. It is never raised above humans, but always takes place with, for, and about others. It emerges in "communicative action" and follows rules, which themselves are always up for discussion. This is even, or especially, true of science. Its knowledge is necessarily provisional, can be challenged and even overturned—which makes it dramatically different than the supposed "absolute knowledge" conferred by religious faith.

Truth, then, can never be the realm of the dogmatic, inflexible demand and the obedient, submissive response. Nor is it the postmodern space occupied by a near-infinity of individual and group points of view. Its spirit is not best imbibed passively, by rote, or by accepting that everyone's claim to truth is as valid as everyone else's. It is generated actively, among people, questioningly, challengingly. To believe in truth is to accept living within this process, to embrace being part of the widest possible human community.

What, then, can we know today? When I started thinking about this chapter, I went around asking friends and acquaintances what they thought were life's most important unanswered questions. The responses were fascinating: How can the world become a better place? After death, will you meet the people from your life who have died? Would I be different if I were born on a different day? What causes envy? Is there life after death? Why in every society are men more violent than women? What is it that makes me myself from one moment to the next? Is para-normal experience possible? Is truly altruistic behavior possible? What is beauty? What causes cancer? What is/ where is/ who is God? Where will I be after death? How do you know if you've chosen the best path for your life? Are we reborn in different forms? Is there a soul that exists separately from the body?

Some of these questions are clearly unanswerable on principle—those about the soul or death or God, for example. Others depend on establishing appropriate frameworks of verifiability—for example, settling on a definition of what would make the world better, or what one means by altruism. Still others should be answerable on principle, such as those about beauty, envy, male violence, and cancer.

After a short while, I became dissatisfied with having asked my friends about life's unanswered questions. My questions encouraged many people to think about life's great mysteries rather than the great achievements of human efforts to make sense of the world. Both are important, of course, but this book has been about living in *this* world. I realized my mistake while watching a PBS program on the human heart that focused on what was learned by the Framingham Study of Risk Factors in Heart Disease. Its first published results, in 1961, revolutionized how we think about heart attacks by confirming the decisive effect of smoking, diet, and lack of exercise. We now *know* all this! We know dozens, hundreds, thousands of things that are vital for human understanding and well-being—have verified, confirmed, and implemented them. In this, the twenty-first century, so much that was once cloaked in darkness is known, and so much that is really essential to our lives is knowable. We sell ourselves short to pretend otherwise. We have developed meth-ods of analysis, synthesis, and reasoning that can be taught and learned. All of this is now part of what Dewey calls the "social consciousness of the race" and it belongs to all of us. It is waiting to be claimed and used.

As a result, either at present or in the foreseeable future, we can know when the earth came into being and how. Why black Americans are poorer than white Americans. How human freedom evolved. How life began. Why cities like Detroit, Manchester, Liverpool, Leipzig, Halle, and Ivanovno have been shrinking for a generation. What people need to have the chance to live better lives. Why creationism flourishes in the United States. How the human brain operates. Why Americans are more religious than people in every other advanced society. How many people the earth can support at an adequate level of subsistence. Why the Holocaust happened. Why Pizarro conquered the Incas and not the Incas Spain. Why Americans are less tall than members of other advanced societies. Why the British were able to dominate massive areas of Africa. Why so much of Africa remains poor today. Why the U.S. murder rate is higher than any other advanced society's. Why Honduras and South Africa have the highest murder rates in the world. Why Greenland and the polar ice caps are melting. Why university costs rise faster than the rate of inflation. How the incredible diversity of plants and animals has evolved from single-celled beings over the last 3.6 billion years. Why Israel is reluctant to make peace with the Palestinians. Why Palestinians are reluctant to make peace with Israel.

We can answer most of these already, and none of the remainder will remain shrouded in mystery forever, or even for very long. Each reader will be able to make a similarly impressive list of life's *answerable* questions. This is the important list. It tells us where we are. It is the one we can use to live our lives and make sense of our world. It is the one from which we can take bearings.

So much knowledge already belongs, or will belong, to the human community.

What can we know, then? An amazing amount if we free ourselves from fears, prejudices, and official stories, and if we develop the disposition to avoid weird beliefs and we learn to make connections. Enough to create a decent life, if we approach the world's growing complexity and its accompanying mountain of information actively and intentionally, determined to make sense of things. Enough to live by—if we choose to know.

Dying
Without God

HOW DO WE LIVE IN THE SHADOW OF DEATH? IF THERE
is no heaven and no afterlife, this life is all there is. Our time
on earth is all we have. Living without God, I have said, we are
not atoms adrift in an absurd universe. We dependent human
creatures are part of the cosmos, nature, and history, as well as
members of local, national, and global society. These dependencies fill our lives with demands, responsibilities, and meaning. How does a person who is aware of this, who shares this
outlook, face death and dying?

I share Robert Solomon's view that it matters far more
to come to terms with our end than to be preoccupied with
"metaphysical speculation" about what might lie beyond this
life. Death is present and palpable, a matter of evidence. Not
only are there no good grounds for anticipating immortality,
but also doing so distracts us from the life that we do have. Individuals concerned with life's meaning, in the here and now, will
ask: How shall we live, knowing that we are going to die? One

time-honored answer for atheists, agnostics, and secularists begins by seeing death as nothing unusual. It is simply the
biologically inevitable end of life, the point at which decisive
physical systems run down so far that the organism itself can no
longer function. If our death is not first brought about by something outside us, or by disease—if we are fortunate, that is—our
bodies themselves will eventually wear out and stop working.
As medical professors have enjoyed pointing out for generations in introductory lectures, dying begins at birth—death is,
after all, the essential precondition of living, the most natural of
processes.

Although this understanding of death is borne out by recent
scientific and medical knowledge, it is also among the oldest
of philosophical approaches. Epicurus said it memorably over
2000 years ago: "Death is nothing to us, since when we are,
death has not come, and when death has come, we are not." It is
not terrible to no longer be alive, because what happens afterward is not judgment, reward, or punishment, but the dispersal
of what were once our atoms. There is nothing to fear. We will
be no more—that is all.

Epicurus hoped that understanding this would take "away
the desire for immortality," and at the very least it has encouraged many people over the generations to live without terror
about supposed punishments in store for them. Scientists have
brought this up to date by learning more and more about how
brain activity is rooted in our physical being. And so, when the
one stops, so does the other. No experientially or scientifically
ascertainable *me* survives my demise. Respect for the contemporary medical understanding of death would have avoided the
public nonsense of the Karen Ann Quinlan and Terry Schiavo
fiascos twenty years apart in the United States, when dead young
women were kept attached to machines because other people
were in denial.

As Ernest Becker would say, the underlying reason for this is that we live in such terror of ourselves no longer existing that we cannot bear to face it. Since Freud, we have developed the intellectual tools for understanding this response. We anticipate with dread the time when we will no longer be, but repress that fear and are tormented by it. Unlike other animals, Becker says, the human creature lives "a whole lifetime with the fate of death haunting one's dreams and even the most sun-filled days." Because grasping this fully is likely to literally "drive us crazy," the most common reaction is the "denial of death." But like other forms of repression diagnosed by Freud, this produces a range of psychic and social pathologies. Becker's *Denial of Death*, winning a Pulitzer Prize in 1974, stimulated research into many aspects of death-denial, notably Robert Jay Lifton's work on "psychic numbing," and has indirectly encouraged the recent movement to confront death openly, including the considerable increase in hospice care and dying at home.

Nothingness and denial: these insights are our starting points. But when each presents itself as the entire answer to living and dying, and we organize our lives around it, it grows less convincing, creating as many problems as it solves. Despite the popular conception of Epicureanism as a form of hedonism, as a philosophy it is really a strategy of minimizing one's needs. Epicurus counsels protecting oneself against pain, insecurity, and frustration by desiring as little as possible so we can face death as if we are nothing but atoms. But the self that we are is more than atoms, more than the sum of our physical components. This center of awareness does not merely get dispersed at our death—it ceases to exist. At my death the particular human adventure that is me, including my consciousness, my psychic life, and my being in the world, will be over.

I fear this end because I want to live, I want to be, not as dispersed atoms but as the self that I am. That self already knows a considerable amount about the nothingness that awaits me, and I resist this, even if I never say a word about it. I know that my mind will stop working, all sensation will cease, I will have no feelings, my power of motion will stop, time will end. From early childhood I have sensed this in killing ants and mosquitoes, in eating dead creatures, in seeing people cease to exist, in noticing my parents mourning, in experiencing painful losses of family members, in sharing in public sadness when important people die. From very early I learn to perceive, along with everyone around me, the end of human life as the most painful loss there is—as life's irresolvable tragedy. Our tears and fears register the momentousness of death, this goodbye from which there is no turning back, even when the person is aged and has lived a full life. By making light of it, Epicureans who argue that "death is nothing" end up, Solomon says, "demeaning life." Thomas Lynch, a funeral director–poet, agrees: "Where death means nothing, life is meaningless." That is, we need to mark the passing of a life, to "close the gap between the death that happens and the death that matters." It is important that witnesses register that something remarkable has ended, "say we lived, we died, we made this difference."

How then to appreciate death? As an effort to confront it, Becker's *Denial of Death* has the opposite weakness. Solomon might have been discussing Becker when criticizing the "death-fetishism" of Heidegger and similar philosophers who make all of life a "being-towards-death." As Solomon says, "just as one can try to ignore it . . . one can also make *too much* out of death." Struggling to undo denial, Becker asserts that what we have been hiding from is life's central dimension. Yes, I agree, it is its most feared one, and yes, its most tenaciously denied one. But is death built into life, or is it life that is built into death? Even as death haunts us, despite our fears we continue to be deeply involved in all the things of life—love, children, learning, work, politics, society, culture, pleasure. They are after all why we live, aren't they?

The fear of death so dominates Becker that he dismisses the possibility of facing it squarely. He points out that Freud confronted the repressed fear of death as a major psychic structure. In fact, Freud contributed one of his most lasting analyses on these themes, seeking to describe the illusory gratification of religion. Becker makes use of Freud's essential discoveries but he turns them on their head by disavowing Freud's atheism. He gives us a stark choice between the believer and the disbeliever, Kierkegaard and Freud, celebrating the first and dismissing the second by psychoanalyzing Freud's own choices. What Becker ends up with, despite his power and insight, is despair about building a decent life with and for our fellow humans, and he turns to religion, which alone "solves the problem of death." While sneering at utopian followers of Freud, Becker extols a vague "heroic" stance in the face of death, promoting his own ideal for overcoming denial: "a lived, compelling illusion that does not lie about life, death, and reality." By this illusion it turns out that he means Christianity.

Although neither gives us a full appreciation of life in the face of dying, their key insights—Epicurus's notion of death as nothing and Becker's theme of the denial of death—do point us in the right direction. They provoke us to encounter the nothingness that awaits us, and to face up to our own impulse to deny that we will die. As psychiatrist Lifton says, "imaginative access to death in its various psychic manifestations is necessary for vitality and vision." Writers and poets have accordingly made death one of the great themes of imaginative literature throughout human history. In various ways they have sought to *live* death, to *live* dying: to think about it, of course, but also to confront, to experience, to imagine, to feel. A great example, Leo Tolstoy's short novel *The Death of Ivan Ilyich*, tells of one man's life and death, and the last thirty pages are an astonishing portrayal of his final days and hours. He has lived steeped in conformity and denial and now he is aware that he is dying, and that others are still pretending to deny this.

> Whether it was morning or evening, Friday or Sunday, made no difference, it was all just the same: the gnawing, unmitigated, agonizing pain, never ceasing for an instant, the consciousness of life inexorably waning but not yet extinguished, the approach of that ever dreaded and hateful Death which was the only reality, and always the same falsity. . . .

The rest of the story is about Ivan Ilych's horrifying and yet ultimately liberating break with the pretense, his deathbed encounter with the meaning of his wasted life.

Albert Camus sought to break through the prevailing denial in a rather different way. Death begins and ends *The Stranger* (a funeral and an execution) and pervades *The Plague* (disease borne by rats kills humans). Most interesting for us, at the beginning of *The Myth of Sisyphus,* Camus paradoxically poses the question of suicide: "There is only one really serious philosophical question, and that is suicide. Deciding whether or not life is worth living is to answer the fundamental question in philosophy. All other questions follow from that." Posing it this way shows that to live or to die is up to us, and we must understand our life as a choice. The point is not only that life must eventually end, but also that if we despair of it we can end it ourselves at any moment. And by deciding to live, we are deciding that our life has value. Sartre's gloss on this is worth noting: "The absurd man will not commit suicide; he wants to live, without relinquishing any of his certainty, without a future, without hope, without illusions, and without resignation either. He stares at death with passionate attention and this fascination liberates him."

Even as we decide to live, death is the nothing that everything presupposes. As such, it casts its shadow on everything we do. We understand implicitly: the condition of all that we are and do is its ultimate cessation. This tragic reality is the very nature of being alive. Death belongs to life itself, even as life wears out here, renews itself there. The young Camus, formulating both his ideas and his literary style, vividly demonstrated this by insisting that "there is no superhuman happiness, no eternity outside of the curve of the days. . . . I can see no point in the happiness of angels." There is nothing but *this* world, *this* life, the present. "The world is beautiful, and outside there is no salvation." In accepting the bitterness and absurdity of death one most intensely appreciates what one *has* and *knows*. And so Camus's famous sensuous and lyrical side, his bathing in the intense and sparkling present, is a demonstration of what life means and feels like to the conscious unbeliever. "I love this life with abandon and wish to speak of it boldly: it makes me proud of my human condition."

We may accept death as inevitable in the long run, but as Darwin understood, most of life organizes itself to combat death or to forestall it. In the human world—the production of food, clothing, shelter, everything pertaining to healthcare, societies coordinating these activities, and everything we create that outlasts an individual's lifespan—all of this stems from and implicitly reminds us of our mortality. In these ways, too, death enters into everything we do. Struggling against it and holding it at bay as long as we can, we live with death at every moment, and life means nothing without its twin.

So can we then understand it, encounter it, become intimate

with it? We may be able to imagine losing sensation and consciousness, the moment before we die, but after briefly trying to imagine nothingness, we then move outside ourselves and watch the person who has died. Freud pointed out the tendency to see ourselves at our own funeral, as if we were a spectator. Sociologist Zygmunt Bauman explains this at length by describing the impossibility of consciousness conceiving of itself as not existing. In a kind of inverted Cartesian cogito, that which is thinking is incapable of thinking that it cannot exist. This logical and psychic impossibility is surrounded by the fact that when we try to think about death itself, we inevitably do so using lenses of our particular society at a particular moment of its historical development.

As all historical and literary explorations of death and dying reveal, our groping for this most rudimentary fact of all, death, leads us to the ways in which this or that specific group of people experience death. For example, the amazing sequence in the Australian movie *Ten Canoes* reconstructs a scene in which an aborigine, in the deep past, dies in the midst of his tribe. He dances his own death dance, then collapses and waits for his father's and grandfather's souls to come fetch him while other warriors take up his dance and sing for him. And then, his body remaining among them but his soul departed, his tribespeople mourn his passing, and settle his affairs.

Why should this portrayal be so compelling to contemporary people living in an advanced society? When death is imaginatively reconstructed, and made accessible to us today, despite our very different lives and kinds of knowledge, we immediately respond. Whatever our religious beliefs, in daily life we rarely live as if we take very seriously the notion that the soul departs from the body when we die. And we have largely lost the ability to affirm our collective existence in dying. Yet we know the end that death is. The ceremony in *Ten Canoes* speaks to us as great poetry from elsewhere or another time: we experience it, even if longingly and from a distance, because as particular as it is, it is also about something universal.

One of the aspects of our life that distinguishes us sharply from earlier societies and other cultures is that today death, the omnipresent force, has become vague and remote to us. Even those who still believe in some kind of an afterlife today usually have only the most foggy and watered-down conception of what it is. Children rarely see a dying person, hear very little talk about death, and as opposed to the past, hear instead only veiled and suggestive references, or vacuous evocations of dead people having entered into heaven. A survey carried out in Sweden recently revealed that, in that most secular and modern of societies, awash like our own in sensitive expert advice and "how-to" knowledge, parents overwhelmingly chose not to discuss a dying child's impending death with that child, although many regretted it afterward. Similarly, in our own society, despite growing advice to the contrary, in the most contemporary of families, children are not exposed to talk of death for fear of upsetting them. The dying are not among them, cemeteries are far away, and the silence about death is pervasive.

In advanced and postindustrial societies, compared with all other cultures at all other times, death is not part of our life. Sociologist Norbert Elias has written suggestively about "the loneliness of the dying." When the experts widely tell us "to introduce the idea of death as a part of everyday life" we can be sure that this is because the opposite is taking place most of the time. A taboo on openly discussing death is common.

Yet despite this dominant tendency, knowledge and understanding have continued to accumulate and are beginning to have an impact in the opposite direction. One of the important early contributions, Jacques Choron's *Modern Man and Mortality*, deserves special mention because it systematically surveys past and recent Western attitudes toward death and dying, with a cross-cultural awareness of other major approaches. Published in 1964, its most important achievement was to clearly distinguish and discuss in detail the different kinds of death fears: of nonexistence, of the moment of dying, of the pain of dying, of an untimely death, and of punishment in an afterlife. Nearly a decade into the twenty-first century, best-selling self-help books are being published about death and dying, courses are being given, and "dying with dignity" has become a contemporary concern. A greater awareness of death as a part of life seems to be making its way into the mainstream. That a successful book was titled *1000 Places to See Before You Die* speaks volumes about this newer tendency. In the United States there has been an increase in the number of people dying at home, as well as a huge jump in the number of hospices. A healthy secular attitude toward death and dying entails continuing this trend and bringing death into our lives more and more consciously.

It may be correct to say that we can never really know death while we are alive and once dead we cannot know it either. And also that we can never leave our social and historical skin and see it "as it is." Still, we do have those moments when our mind turns a corner and we suddenly sense that we are going to die. There are times when we look at ourselves in the mirror and see lines in our face that we never noticed before, when we run to catch a bus or train and feel an unexpected sense of strain or shortness of breath. After we reach middle age, it is undeniable that we are running down. We try to remember an embarrassingly familiar person's name at a party but it eludes us as we desperately struggle to cover up. We forget what we came into the room to get, we can no longer follow certain kinds of complex arguments. We hear ourselves sliding over words as our articulation becomes less precise. And once again we glimpse our death, this time imagining our grandchildren forgetting us, our children mourning us, our spouse alone, or our house sitting empty without us.

Yes, it may be impossible to fully conceive ourselves not being here, and perhaps we cannot avoid some denial, but we do have dozens of intimations, hints, and feelings, including matter-of-fact moments, times of surprise and shock, terrifying encounters, unspeakable sadness, incurable moods of loss. We sense our death as an irresolvable tragedy. It is the utter end, without appeal. It may be unthinkable and unutterable, but it is the absolute brute fact we have been holding off as long as possible, and we know this absolutely.

Does honoring such times of feeling, imagining, and thinking, rather than ignoring or running from them, risk incapacitating us and rendering us unable to live our lives? On the contrary, as Lifton tells us, it is among the life-affirming things we can do. Still, why make it into a lifelong project rather than trying to think through and answer its key questions once and for all? Because knowledge of death is contingent and partial, like all matters of truth and knowing. Our concerns about it will change as we change, recurring until the day we die. Does dealing with death threaten us with confusion and distraction? On the contrary, it clarifies our life to be aware that it ends. Why can't we avail ourselves of social wisdom, time-honored cultural patterns of dealing with death? Because those few that are still accessible to us are mostly steeped in denial. As it turns out, in facing death we are undertaking a characteristically modern task:

becoming as conscious as possible, using contemporary insights and knowledge, and doing so on our own, frequently revisiting and revising our thoughts and feelings.

These questions and these answers may be troubling and demanding, and accordingly they feed into perhaps the most common form of resistance: we think there is still time to deal with issues of death and dying. What after all is the urgency of beclouding ourselves with troubling thoughts now? It is well known that when Becker wrote *The Denial of Death*, although not yet fifty, he was dying of cancer. And his own sense of urgency is palpable on every page. But don't most of us have at least a little more time before it is absolutely necessary to take up these end-of-life questions?

Nietzsche's remarks can guide us: the goal of encountering death is that we may "say yes to life." If living without God means anything today, it means living as completely as possible, every day of our lives, experiencing all that there is to experience, freeing oneself from obstacles in doing so. At bottom, I want to encourage our having the fullest possible awareness of our place in the universe, our belonging, our dependency, our responsibility. I want to encourage our seeing and experiencing life as fully as we can. If this was as true of our guilt and resentments as of our gratitude, of our complicity as our power to rupture with it, it is no less true of our dread of death. The point of Nietzsche's statement is that to be wholly alive means being as aware of the negative as of the positive. It demands feeling life's pain. As he advised, saying yes to life means not shunning any experience, embracing it "even in its strangest and most painful episodes."

Michael Roemer's film *Dying* powerfully shows that all that may be left to us is no more and no less than living one's last days by experiencing them completely, including mourning and saying goodbye. The film concentrates on three persons' final illnesses. Sally, come home to die with brain cancer, whose life seems as if it may have been wasted, was able to share her last moments with her elderly mother while bravely facing the end. Their quiet, accepting last months together are denied to a young married couple, Bill and Harriet. Harriet's anger and loss about being left with two young children make them unable/unwilling to feel their pain and anger freely and to share it with each other. Crippled by denial, not able to mourn openly as Bill lives through his last days with lymphoma, their loss is total. The film's third subject, Reverend Bryant, pastor of a black Baptist church, talks openly about his cancer during a sermon. He dies with his family gathered around him, including his grandchildren. With the beauty of a life fully lived and a loss fully felt, his death is paradoxically life-affirming because the pain is shared openly, collectively. His case shows us that a religious death can be among the best of all deaths. It suggests a kind of grace in death that unbelievers seek without religion, encouraging us to encounter—yes, even embrace—death directly and fully, surrounded by a loving family and community.

Through Sally's and Reverend Bryant's deaths and their contrast with Bill and Harriet's terrible story, *Dying* teaches us that mourning and saying goodbye are among the most important ways of saying yes to life, because doing so means fully living its most painful moment. But, as it turns out, we must not do this just once, but dozens of times before our end, as we grow and decline through life's stages, and as we lose loved ones. Many painful moments lie along our own paths through life—which reveal common patterns, for example among this author's cohort, middle-class white males living in this society today. In our twenties and thirties we may have had either a vague or a sharp awareness of life's irreversibility—no longer being a child, no longer starting out in life, no longer finding our way. In our forties this commonly yields to the "midlife crisis" of realizing that our life has its shape, and the features that displease us are not so easily separated from those that please us. If we were fortunate, the awareness of decline was postponed until our fifties, with only the death of parents, the occasional death of a friend, or a serious illness to remind us of our own mortality. But beginning in our fifties, and then certainly by our sixties, no matter who we are, our physical changes—the markers of decline—are impossible to ignore.

By seventy—this writer's age at the publication of this book—one can draw up a list of the signs of aging. Everyone's will be slightly different, but by the beginning of our eighth decade it may certainly include trembling hands, memory loss, hearing loss, loss of hair color, deteriorating eyesight, a lengthening nose, loss of fullness in the face, loss of height, pains that won't go away, medical conditions needing constant medication or other therapeutic intervention, more frequent and lasting tiredness, loss of strength, loss of physical stamina, speech becoming less precise, urinary complications, sexual dysfunction, sleep disruptions, and more frequent muscular stiffness. And, of course, one of the most terrifying faces of death today, cancer. What does it mean to call these "signs of aging"? We are functioning less optimally because our bodies are wearing down—as one friend said, we have accumulated "a lot of miles." The automotive metaphor is charged with an awareness that our machinery cannot continue to run endlessly, that it is in the process of wearing out, that death awaits us, we are inching closer to it. By one's eighth decade this awareness becomes our constant companion.

If being obsessively aware of this at every moment, like Woody Allen's Mickey Sachs in *Hannah and Her Sisters*, is making a fetish of death, being unaware of it is denying death. Each person will have their own best way of facing death, but I am arguing that this includes allowing oneself to work through its many different aspects. Working through means living through times of loss, loneliness, sadness, emptiness, dread, fear, and mourning. In other words, at various times and ways in one's life, and more frequently as one ages, death will enter one's consciousness, and such thoughts and feelings must be honored. We know that it is possible to hide from these, and that they can be ignored. But, to speak in the imperative, there is really no hiding from them: they must be lived.

We are always, in a sense, answering death, this nothing that conditions everything. One of the responses to death, and our lesson from Nietzsche, is to experience life. To honor our feelings about death in our twenties, thirties, or forties is to sense them connected with a restless fear of not living all the way. At twenty, I recall listening to two very good men in their forties, a record shop owner and a record company salesman, talking sadly about how they had failed to realize their youthful hopes, the one to study music, the other to become an actor. Their regrets said to me: How important is it to live fully rather than face the ache of not having lived!

If we are aware that we only have this life, we may experience this awareness with some urgency. It does not have to become an exhausting demand that every moment must be lived to its limit. But it can result in the determination to not let one's life be dominated by the undone. It can result in taking chances that one has avoided, or deciding to contribute to the world after all. By itself, avoiding regret is obviously not a complete life strategy, but it points to the crucial difference between living fully and not doing so. Regret is a first possible response to the awareness

of death, and contains at least a half-consciousness that we cannot help judging ourselves and our lives, that we will eventually
have to answer—to ourselves—how we live our time and use our
energies. Will we be satisfied with what we have done, or will we
regret not having been fully alive?

"Not being fully alive" is such a common expression that we
ignore how strange and paradoxical it is. The same is true of
talk about "feeling dead." Why do we so often use such ultimate
metaphors to describe daily-life feelings and experiences? Of
course there is the disposition to exaggerate. But are we making a
far-fetched comparison with what one imagines death to be like,
or is there something actually deathlike in the experience?

It is significant that we feel more dead at one moment, more
alive at another. Obviously, words matter. We deaden ourselves
when we anesthetize our feelings and our awareness in certain
stressful situations—numbing ourselves to our own experience.
Unable to keep from feeling pain or being troubled, we do the
next best thing—repress. We make something not exist for ourselves by making ourselves not exist to it. We avoid it by making
that part of ourselves go dead. Why "dead"? Because we move
into a state of reduced vital energy, emotion, consciousness,
intellect, and activity. At the moment, we pretend that we don't
exist as a strategy for coping with the discomfort of existence.
We act as if we don't feel, hear, or think.

Our positive talk about being "fully alive" suggests that we
value living our lives in such a way as to minimize such states
of feeling deadened and maximize the times when our intense
energies and feelings flow through us. This means remaining
alert to what is taking place around us and within us, using our
capacities to their utmost—at work, in relationships, as citizens,
and in play. Thinking about one individual living with greater
awareness, vitality, and emotion, and feeling sorry for another

living with less, we sense that the first has "more life" than the second. We admire the individual who has energy, develops her capacities, and achieves, and we conclude that she is living well.

Whatever kind of life we are creating, it still leads, if we are fortunate, to old age. If we are fortunate, we avoid a violent death, dying by accident, or dying by disease. And then we have those everyday worries: losing our teeth, wetting our pants, not following what someone is saying, the pain in our back, neck, or hip making it harder to move, younger people growing impatient with us for needing them to repeat what they say, straining to stay connected to the world, fearing that we will become irrelevant and then invisible. Even if we have few regrets about how we have spent our life, we feel ourselves slipping away.

The people closest to us share our pained awareness, observing us from the point of view of our decline, of how we used to be and what we can no longer do, fretting over our mental lapses and hesitations and physical weaknesses, annoyed by our passing enthusiasms, tallying silently, as we do, what we are giving up. We can no longer run, no longer play sports, no longer have sex without pharmaceutical assistance, no longer drive a car, no longer walk very far. We tell ourselves that this is temporary, we will try again, but we slowly grow used to our limitations. Sadness and loss can become one's entire perspective on aging.

But to do this would be a serious mistake. It makes it difficult to appreciate and live what remains. Too much sorrow, loss, and "I used to be able to . . ." impede living what is left for us in the present.

As we age, much of who we are resides in our expectations of what we can do, based on remembering what we've been able to do. A diminishment of this or that ability must be absorbed, and in order to live in the present we must redefine our expectations. How we absorb our decline and live in the present is definitive. I recall my aging father, standing in the kitchen, remarking: "In my mind I still feel as young as I always did." In hearing this, his unsympathetic son thought he was just consoling himself. Only now do I realize what I missed then: he was exulting. Aging didn't cancel out his sense of himself, and this remained constant from his earliest childhood until this moment: "I am still who I always was." He was experiencing a deeper "I" than any particular capacity, and was feeling it in the present. He was sensing himself fully alive, despite his losses. At that moment, "I used to be able to . . ." disappeared.

Sometimes one's friends and family will not let this happen. They are attached to what we were, have grown mournful of what we have become, and are now often burdened with the tasks of caring for this aging person. As a result, loved ones may have the greatest difficulty experiencing our aging. The story of Jean-Paul Sartre's last days is remarkable because at the end there seemed to be two Sartres, the fading shadow of the former genius and the still-engaged philosopher willing to rethink everything. The first, loved and tolerated by "la famille" consisting of Simone de Beauvoir and his oldest friends, had become blind, was scarcely able to walk, required constant care, wet his pants, and had given up writing. His life work was behind him, his genius was spent, and these loved ones felt that he had to be protected from being embarrassed by his foolish enthusiasms of the moment. The second Sartre was the man living in the present, the Sartre who was spending time with the young, intense, and ambitious Benny Lévy—taping fresh interviews, revising his old ideas, the two sharply disagreeing then agreeing, going in new directions, together creating the rough outlines of new thoughts.

While Beauvoir tenderly but patronizingly ministered to the fading genius and tried to keep the accumulated works and past accomplishments of her life companion alive and definitive, Sartre wanted to live in the present with Lévy, thinking however crudely and rapidly for hours on tape, looking to the future, engaging in yet one more adventure. Sartre felt, against his oldest loved ones, that this experience, living in the present, mattered most. And in order to not be frozen into the past, keen on turning his remaining abilities to new tasks, wanting passionately to be pointed toward the future, Sartre was to risk an end-of-life rupture with the members of "la famille."

A few years earlier, Simone de Beauvoir had published a study similar in ambition and length to her classic, *The Second Sex*, and it became translated in the United States as *The Coming of Age*. This title is a serious misrepresentation: the implication of growing into someone positive was the exact opposite of what Beauvoir had in mind. The French title was simpler and more straightforward: *La Vieillesse*, and the title of the British translation rendered it honestly: *Old Age*. In this sociological, historical, philosophical, economic, and medical treatise, Beauvoir depicts aging, with rare exceptions, as a time of utter loss. Those few individuals who struggle against their decay "often become caricatures of themselves." There are reasons for this, and Beauvoir's great achievement in this book is to raise consciousness about the social and historical dimensions of aging. Her first point is about modern societies' structures of class and privilege, which eventually but relentlessly produce a huge difference between those who have been fortunate enough to live—and age—well and those who have not. Second, attitudes and policies elbow the aging to the margins of community life, telling them that they no longer matter—indeed, make them no longer matter. By the time they reach old age, the gap between the well-cared-for few and the many who have undergone "systematic destruction" becomes truly enormous. Her indictment and call to arms could not be stronger: "Old age exposes the failure of our entire civilization."

On an even more fundamental—that is to say, biological—level, and even among those who avoid dying due to violence, accident, illness, or disease, the deterioration of old age takes away one's practical activity in the world, one's ability to remain relevant and productive, to contribute socially. The only way to keep old age from becoming an "absurd parody of our former life" is "to go on pursuing ends that give our existence a meaning—devotion to individuals, to groups or to causes, social, political, or intellectual work." But we only accomplish this through a determined act of resistance, both against the aging process itself and the invisible ghetto in which the elderly are placed. Only a very few are able to do this. Since it is our projects that mark fruitful living, our losing the capacity to do them at our accustomed level almost universally makes aging an unmitigated disaster. Even a Michelangelo, creative to the very last, was racked with pain and a sense of loss, and then, in another tragedy of aging, came to disparage his own great statues as "puppets." In old age, he repudiated his achievement. In such cases, we cannot help wondering if death is not preferable to an ending in which "life unravels stitch by stitch like a frayed piece of knitting, leaving nothing but the meaningless strands of wool in the old person's hands."

Beauvoir does acknowledge that the "sweeping away of fetishes and illusions is the truest, most worthwhile of all the contributions of age," but she still ties this "questioning, challenging state of mind" to remaining effective in the world—and in any case does not pursue this new attitude far into old age. Contrary to Beauvoir, what if we look closely at possible consolations of

aging? For some people the list of losses can for some time be off-
set by a number of gains, including a lessening of inner conflict,
greater mental clarity, the ability to make decisions more
easily, freedom from stress, a softening of personality traits that
make life troubling such as ambition, self-consciousness, and
paranoia. With age can come a long-term perspective, greater
calm, a stronger appreciation and caring for other people. Freed
from the heaviest burdens of work, one has time to return to
those treasured and longed-for activities that one has put off all
one's life, to live in the moment listening to music, birdwatch-
ing, gardening, passing time with friends, reading, or dozens of
other heretofore pointless pleasures. This stage of life makes
possible an entirely new way of relating to people, typified in
the unconditional love and carefree pleasure characteristic of a
grandparent.

To Beauvoir all this marks defeat, a giving in to decline and
weakening. She is aware that for a time workers may improve
as they get older, usually during their fifties and sixties. Later
on, life is overwhelmingly a story of losses. Her book reads as
an unflinching compilation of such losses, written against the
disposition to console ourselves. And so she scornfully rejects
the notion of "serenity" accompanying aging. She rejects the
thought of shifting gears from a life centered on one's social
contribution to a less forceful life in which one pursues activities
more and more for their own sake. Living in and for the moment
with weakened capacities is an unworthy replacement for living
in and for one's projects.

To move in the direction I suggest obviously requires a radical shift in perspective, yes, perhaps even an acceptance that
one has little more to do or say or accomplish in the world. Or
even that the wish to do so has faded, that one has contributed
enough in one's lifetime. Is this a tragedy? From a point of view

that refuses to honor any activity but being socially productive, it certainly is. As it is from a point of view that assigns little value to acting at a level of competence weaker than that of the peak of one's mature years. If the essence of adult life is accomplishment and the power to make a difference, living on without these is indeed tragic.

I agree with Beauvoir that resistance should accompany aging: resisting the loss of capacities by exercising them, and refusing to be cast aside by society. These may involve personal, collective, and political projects. In fact the baby boomer generation has become actively engaged in such resistance, the watchword of which is "successful aging." This approach rejects "usual aging" and insists instead that "we can, and should, strive for longer, healthier, more productive lives." By eating well, exercising, and remaining engaged in life, we can live longer and "attain high-quality, vital, disease-free late years." Carried beyond the individual to the realm of social policy, resistance to death can also involve a kind of massive public assault on disease, isolation, and insecurity that Beauvoir was hoping to motivate.

Yet, important as they are, both the all-out resistance to aging that she advocates and the "successful aging" movement of the baby boomers contain their own kind of denial. There is a rejection of life in refusing to adapt or accept ourselves as we change and become diminished, or in scorning living fully in the ways left to us. For all their strengths, Beauvoir and "successful aging" are fixed on the image of the independent, active, productive worker and contributor to society, and are at a loss when faced with the dependent, diseased, weakened souls afflicted by "usual aging." Yes, of course, such losses are genuine, and from the perspective of what once was, they are also tragic. If they can be forestalled, by all means we should do so.

But life's stages each have their own validity. Why not embrace

life on its own terms, and accept that these are constantly changing? It is important to live as fully as possible, but what this
means changes as we move from the beginning of old age to the
end of life. As long as we live, we continue to make ourselves.
The space within which we do so may shrink, but the fact that
we do so continues until the end. Old age offers not only its own
pleasures and consolations, but also the space and need for doing
some of life's most serious work. Granted, this requires being
fortunate enough to have sufficient mental acuity and health,
and often people lack one or both as they near death. Still, an
essential part of living is taking leave. It always has been: Sartre's
last conversation with Lévy, the death dance in *Ten Canoes*, and
Reverend Bryant's last hours are only a few instances in a vast
literature. These endings suggest that summing up, settling our
affairs, and saying goodbye can begin years before we die, and in
fact the sense of self-judgment starting in youth may be more or
less continuous in most people.

Am I a good father? Friend? Mate? Citizen? Am I living fully?
Am I making good use of my abilities? Am I acting morally? Am
I acting to make the world a better place? These are only a few of
the self-judgment questions that we ask frequently. Dying without God injects into them the urgency of a life that is irreversible
and final. An end-of-life judgment entails replacing the present
tense with the past tense: Have I . . . ? The answer is a conclusion
with no appeal to a different future. It is our last judgment, and
any secular version of this simply stands the religious theme, of
being judged by God after our death, back on its feet, acknowledging its real source—ourselves.

Whether or not we actually pass judgment on our life in
a deathbed scene, by one's last days such questions find final
answers. Or almost. The fact is that life is never over until our last

breath, and so even a tortured and long-suppressed awareness of futility, or of insufficiency, or of guilt, or of unresolved anger, or of self-pity, still allows for—what? If our minds and our feelings are lucid, two things remain possible, if not likely, even at the end of life: understanding and forgiveness.

For all one's insufficiencies, and all the unresolved conflicts of a lifetime, it remains possible to understand that we and others have done what we did for reasons. Our life's shape can be explained. We have made ourselves, using materials that we did not provide and under conditions beyond our control. We need not understand every detail, but it is up to us both to take ownership of our creation, this life of ours, and to understand how far it was and was not of our making. It is good to see what we have become and done. And that there were compelling reasons why we avoided following our heart, or ignored some of our responsibilities, or played it safe, or acted in ways we weren't proud of. When we grasp this, pride and shame, both essential, can give way to self-understanding. My record shop owner and record company salesman didn't follow their deepest longings because of the pressures of their lives (including parents to care for and families to support), and so probably found among their life paths fewer possibilities and opportunities than those available to the young man who heard them commiserating. People make themselves, under conditions they didn't make. It is possible to understand this, to accept it, and to forgive it, at any moment of one's life.

Is it possible, then, even on one's deathbed, even in one's last moments, to see and feel what one has missed all one's life, to lift the veil of fear and inhibition that has kept one from living freely, and however briefly to understand and forgive oneself, becoming intensely alive? Even where one's life has been a sad waste, such a flash of reversal, or even a moment of insight, might always be possible, just as it has been possible throughout one's lifetime.

"What if my whole life has really been wrong?" is the question that Ivan Ilych could no longer keep down. A few moments of comfort and caring, given to him by the young servant Gerasim, met a deep need and went against the current of dutiful coldness and pretense Ivan Ilych lived with his family. Just reflecting to himself on the question, with his wife standing over him, pointed to the answer: "This is wrong, it is not as it should be. All you have lived for and still live for is falsehood and deception, hiding life and death from you." This startling admission was followed by three days of horrible screams.

If we are near the end, what does such awareness matter? Ivan Ilych says: "I am leaving this life with the consciousness that I have lost all that was given me and it is impossible to rectify it—what then?" One obvious answer to his question is that such consciousness does not matter. It does not affect the rest of our accumulated life activity, whatever we did or didn't do, because it is almost over. Nor does it change things for those we are close to, who are saying their sad goodbyes, or the world we are leaving. Tolstoy rejected this resignation, refused to allow Ilych to deaden himself, to carry out one last act of psychic numbing, to say no to life to the very end.

We all know people who have done the contrary, even in the slightest of ways, and who manage to change and live differently, even if not dramatically so, as they age. What does it matter? After his three days of screaming for having wasted his life and lived wrongly, Ivan Ilych asks himself: "But what *is* the right thing?" And he "suddenly grew quiet." His schoolboy son was with him, crying and kissing his hand. His wife had entered the room, in tears. He realized that he was making them miserable

and felt sorry for them; it was time to take leave of them. Whatever religious meanings Ivan Ilych's last two hours might have
had for Tolstoy, the greatness of the story rests on its powerful
secular conclusion: Ivan Ilych finds peace only at the very end,
after letting into consciousness the searing awareness of his life's
waste and emptiness, and through momentarily experiencing
and expressing the human tenderness he had always repressed.
His dreadful life ends in a moment of dramatic reversal.

Does it matter? A second example, this one historical, will
also help us answer the question in a different way. "What will
it matter?" must have been the objection raised by many of the
remaining fifty to seventy thousand Jews in the Warsaw Ghetto
who organized resistance in mid-January 1943, as the Germans
began what they thought would be the final evacuation. Until
that point, the Germans, with their customary ruthless efficiency,
had removed most of the several hundreds of thousands of the
Jews they had sealed into the ghetto, shipping them to extermination camps. The prospect of resistance posed a dilemma for
each individual. The Germans promised that the Jews would be
deported to labor camps; perhaps they were telling the truth? Or
might one hide inside the ghetto as the Germans were evacuat-
ing everyone else? Or perhaps it was possible to find a way out to
the "Aryan" side and hide there. Any resistance now would only
briefly delay certain death, perhaps make it even more painful.
And what difference would it make? But now, almost at the end,
Jewish combat groups mobilized and responded by attacking
and killing several of the soldiers assigned to remove Jews.

The Germans withdrew and then methodically organized
what was to be the decisive assault by two thousand troops,
which began on April 19. A force of some fifteen hundred mostly
young and militant Jews attacked the shocked soldiers as they re-
entered, and soon a full-scale battle ensued. It lasted not simply

for a few hours but went on for days and weeks. The stunned Germans, who had counted on liquidating the ghetto in three days, became furious, then desperate, bringing in massive force and setting the ghetto aflame. Yet it still took until the middle of May for the resistance to peter out. Almost all of the Jewish fighters lay dead, a few survivors joined the noncombatants who were shipped to concentration camps, and a few others escaped into Warsaw or out of the city through the sewers.

What difference did it make? The ghetto was razed. A handful lived to tell the story. Their hopeless last-minute transformation into an organized fighting force at least allowed those who resisted to not go willingly, but rather to go down fighting. Dying as combatants, living the last weeks of their lives shooting at German soldiers rather than as victims, made a difference. Moreover, they revealed that the heretofore invincible Germans were vulnerable. Prisoners at places like Treblinka, encouraged by news of the Warsaw Ghetto uprising, organized themselves to destroy their extermination camps. One hopeless act of courage led to others. And now, in the next century, their unforgettable example still has the power to affect and inspire us.

Like the Warsaw Ghetto uprising, does the kind of end-of-life change, seen dramatically on Ivan Ilych's deathbed, make a difference to the person who undergoes it? We know that the fighters of the Warsaw Ghetto, once they entered into combat, exulted in their few moments of active struggle. For those involved, any sort of turnabout can change the meaning of everything that preceded it. A history of passivity, things undone, and missed chances, now becomes the slow, difficult preparation for a last-ditch breakthrough. As we read both fiction and history, we know that such a breakthrough can have an amazing effect on those who witness it or hear about it. And, at a greater distance, that it can become a goad or a model for those who hear about it later. Yes, no matter how late it happens, it makes a difference.

The unlikely examples also suggest that a last-minute self-transformation in the face of death depends on having the energy to undertake it. As one nears the end of life, this requires a kind of double lucidity—of intellectual capacity and emotional honesty. Ivan Ilych was only forty-five, and in full possession of his faculties. Thus it is necessary to repeat, one more time, the qualification I've been insisting on again and again about aging: if we are fortunate. This expresses how precarious is each person's individual pathway to aging and dying, and how much depends on avoiding debilitating illness. "If we are fortunate" also returns us to Beauvoir's concern that our well-being depends in significant ways on historical and social forces well beyond our control. It means avoiding an untimely death in the first place due to violence, suicide, accident, or disease. Just getting to old age depends on having adequate caring, nutrition, and healthcare, and being free of stresses and insecurities that generate despair, shorten one's life, or sap one's vitality. Being able to live to a ripe age means being provided for, avoiding society's scrap heap, and having the freedom and the energy to choose our activities freely, including meaningful work and satisfying play. "If we are fortunate," then, is a recognition that many aren't so fortunate, and that being so is not up to us.

Our own personal sense of vulnerability, and our hope that our healthy years last as long as possible, should not keep us from looking clearly at the larger historical and social issue raised by Simone de Beauvoir, which is civilization's attitude toward death. In *Eros and Civilization*, Herbert Marcuse rejects all efforts to dismiss Freud's "death instinct," because our society, having come to depend on death, retains it as an "instinctual goal." We live as if under the spell of death, because life is so painful. "In a repressive civilization, death itself becomes an instrument of repression. Whether death is feared as constant threat, or glorified as supreme sacrifice, or accepted as fate, the education for consent to death introduces an element of surrender into life from the beginning—surrender and submission."

But there is an alternative, however utopian it may sound. As Marcuse puts it, "under conditions of a truly human existence," we might strive for "dying a 'natural' death after a fulfilled life." Why put quotation marks around "natural"? He stresses that death, like other necessities of life, "can be made rational— painless." People, "after a fulfilled life," "may take it upon themselves to die—at a moment of their own choosing." By this he suggests the possibility of a kind of old age and dying different than most of humanity has known for all of its history.

The qualifications surrounding this vision are important. He is speaking about the societal and civilizational level: this kind of death should be available to everyone after living a life of fulfillment, which should also be available to everyone. Achieving both would require a revolutionary effort to reverse the basic direction of a civilization that is built on toil, exploitation, domination, and repression. The painful death of the victims of past generations, ending painful lives, remains the norm of the present, and "the accumulated guilt of mankind against its victims" haunts us all and helps keep us from breaking free.

In contrast, the citizens of a nonrepressive civilization would protest with all their might against death and dying. What Marcuse has in mind, and for which he openly claims the label of "utopian" that Becker will scorn, is literally a societal struggle against death. But in the fifty years since Marcuse wrote *Eros and Civilization,* hasn't this been taking place? After all, enormous social investment in every advanced society goes toward warding off death—efforts to combat prostate cancer, for example, have produced ever-more-sophisticated modes of screening, several different forms of treatment, and considerable attention to minimizing and managing the side effects of treatment. The wealthiest nations have become committed on many fronts to making life longer and more healthful.

I suspect that Marcuse would still regard ours as a minimal commitment and a scanty investment, geared to a privileged sector of humanity, barely more than a politically necessary lip service hiding a deeper and darker reality. To understand this, we need only imagine what humanity's "greatest struggle" would look like. It would have two seemingly contradictory aspects, both of which run contrary to current practice: combating death, and accepting it. The first would entail a relentless and world-wide campaign, beyond anything glimpsed so far, to lengthen life for everyone—not only making aging more protected, but providing the resources to make life more secure and satisfying for all. This might include intensive worldwide efforts to promote public health beginning with conception and childbirth, campaigns to reduce murders and accidents, and truly massive global efforts to avoid and eliminate disease, as well as huge social investments in the well-being of the aged. To do this, everyone's life—and thus everyone's well-being—would have to be taken far more seriously than at present. And this would presuppose a successful struggle to end the various forms of inequality and domination prevailing in the world today. Marcuse is asking us to imagine a full-scale social mobilization against death and poverty on behalf of a radical goal: that all of humanity is entitled to live well. This would draw not merely upon skills and financial resources, but also upon "the unrepressed energy" of the whole population.

Making the conditions of life satisfying for all might mean that people would no longer feel the need to cling to it senselessly when it is effectively over. Assuming that societal resources will always be limited, we will have to face the implications of the choice we are currently making: to keep some people alive at all costs in the advanced world drains resources from combating epidemics and diseases that are running rampant in impoverished countries. Americans are all potential Karen Quinlans and Terry Schiavos in a world of dying children. Changing our outlook on such issues is less a matter of updating medical ethics to harmonize with new lifesaving technologies than of implementing global norms of equality: freeing life everywhere from toil, poverty, resignation, and submission to inhuman forces like "the bottom line." In other words, global society's goal would become overcoming the barriers everywhere to devoting our technological and scientific capacities to the "pacification of existence."

At a certain point, to use one of Marcuse's favorite expressions, quantity turns into quality: now feeling secure about living out our full lifespan at a high level of satisfaction and well-being, individuals might sense death itself differently, not as a dreaded yet longed-for cessation of a painful life, but as something to be freely chosen when life is no longer worth living. In such conditions, which would amount to a civilizational transformation, "death can become a token of freedom."

To return from the future to the present, from the societal to the personal, from a utopian vision of death to the reality of our individual dying, Marcuse provides a caution that applies to each one of us today. Individuals "can die without anxiety if they know that what they love is protected from misery and oblivion." Although today's watchword of "dying with dignity" has evolved as a personal and family goal, containing no wider social vision, an essential goal of anyone's final moments would be to die without anxiety in the sense Marcuse is referring to.

Here is where the personal again becomes social and historical in a way that must not be ignored. The world is wracked with pain that is nowhere near being eased. As the capacities for alleviating the struggle for survival have increased, the misuse of these capacities only becomes more irrational. Why irrational? Because such a social order is functioning against itself and its deepest goals. It pretends that we are not interdependent, that the resources we consume and claim as our own in order to live well are not ultimately global resources. It is irrational because a life of well-being over here drains those who live poorly over there. It is irrational because a security that depends on someone else's insecurity can never rest easy.

We are patently unable to take our leave with any sense of security about what will survive us. It is difficult to rest easy as human social progress becomes harder to discern each year, as the world presents us with more and more reasons to be gloomy about its direction after we are gone. All our exertions have been unable to protect what we love, both the people and the purposes to which we have devoted ourselves. This is the tragedy lurking around the edges of even the best-lived life. We are unable to die in peace.

Our situation will be even worse if we have evaded our responsibilities. We may seek to die in the illusion that our life was only about us and a very narrow circle of devotion, and not about a lifetime of belonging to and participating in the wider world. If we've devoted ourselves to making this world a better place, at least we may have spared ourselves the guilt of colluding with its continuing evils and worsening trends, or the "loneliness of dying" Norbert Elias speaks of, or the saccharine pretense that nothing in our life has mattered but loving and obeying the Ten Commandments. Even if we have been committed and active on behalf of the kinds of goals suggested in this book, we may still feel the pain of leaving a world that is no better than when we entered it. But at least we will feel the fullness of our belonging to it as we depart, and of having put our best into it.

And after we are gone, what is left of us? When philosopher Jacques Derrida was interviewed during the last days of his life, he spoke about "survival"—whatever remains after our death of our life activity and contributions. Robert Jay Lifton develops a more systematic analysis of ways in which we seek "symbolic immortality." However we describe it, after we are dead, the fact is that we will "live on" in large ways and small. I have shown some large ways throughout this chapter, everywhere referring to dead writers in terms of what they "say" to us in the present tense, rather than what they "said" while they were alive. I most specifically have in mind Robert Solomon, who died while I was working on this book, but whose work is important for me, and Herbert Marcuse, who was my teacher, and to whose writings I have returned several times over my lifetime. But this is no less true for Plato, Epicurus, Freud, Becker, Tolstoy, Camus, Sartre, or Beauvoir: they continue to speak to us today. They are long since dead, but something of what they did—indeed, something of them—survives into the present, and we live with it.

This is not only true of writers and their books, or of people whose influence on us we are accustomed to notice, such as our parents. It is worth taking the time to reflect on how, in large ways and small, attitudes, actions, and decisions of those who came before us, and those who continue to live around us, affect us and make us who we are. This is a dimension of our being that calls for being mapped as we become more fully aware of our dependencies, our responsibilities, and ourselves. A major role in my life and identity was played by grandparents I never knew, a forgotten one who died when I was three, and step-grandparents whose love I remember. Most of them left me fragments to go on, from old photographs and stories—glints of pride, moments of conviction, acts of freedom, and specific decisions—all of which continue to affect me today, two generations later.

And I will have my own effect, into the future. Houses we have built and bought and lived in survive us, trees we have planted survive us, public edifices built with our tax money survive us, the contributions of our working lives survive us; people we have given of ourselves to, and our children and theirs, survive us. Just as our grandparents and parents remain with us for our entire lives, so may something of us remain with our loved ones far into the future. I do not mean simply being remembered. My grandson will not recall those many nights during his first six months, when I calmed his colic by dancing with him until he fell asleep. With his father away in military service because of the war in Iraq, he had special need of his grandfather's love, and it became part of him.

Many of the most important effects people have upon each other enter unconsciously into their personalities and characters—indeed, into their bearing and posture and ways of moving through life, becoming absorbed into who they are. My daughter, Pamela Aronson, demonstrates this in an essay she wrote. She points out how, in the case of feminism, the results of social struggles become absorbed into the identities of those who come afterward. These struggles, and their victories, continue to be lived, even when the subsequent generations are without any awareness of the ideas and movements that originally generated their own attitudes and prospects.

Most people don't pay attention to vital facts like these, but to the extent that this book, and especially this chapter, survives me, Dave Wagner and Chris Felcyn, the genial morning classical music hosts of Detroit radio station WRCJ-FM, will live on in it for their delightful conversation and soothing programming as I wrote this during the trying summer of 2007. I make these acknowledgments part of the text itself, and there could be many others, to show that we all live on in others in elemental ways, through our disposition, our example, our caring, our sense of humor, our way of solving problems, as well as through our conscious and deliberate contributions. We live on through the memory of special moments in which we were present. And we live on through being a grain of sand in the vast social movements that we lived through and in which we participated. What we have done, and who we have been, remains part of the wider universe long after we are gone. This is only one of many things we might hope to affirm in the face of death.

Hope

NOW THAT THE RIVERWALK IS OPEN, AND DOWNTOWN Detroit has a delightful path for exercising, strolling, or looking around, I go there eagerly, after breakfast. The sights include the General Motors Building, one of the world's tallest hotels, a memorial to the Underground Railroad, and the skyline of Windsor, Canada, less than a mile across the river. I am grateful for this continually expanding promenade, which is destined to attract new homes and shops as well as walkers. It is a center-piece in the rebuilding of downtown Detroit, which has finally gathered enough momentum, after years of sputtering, to be self-generating. At first I'm the only person out on this gray fall morning, and I am slightly apprehensive about being here alone. I know the city's reputation for crime, and the reality it is based on, but still I have always insisted on walking in the city where I was born. Soon more people come out and I relax. While walking, a few usual minor concerns crop up—my arthritic hip hurts a little, I'm aware of a slight pain in my knee, and I didn't gauge the nearest men's room carefully enough. Still, for a native Detroiter this three-mile walk combines a long-awaited pleasure with hope for the city's future.

In the first chapter I posed Immanuel Kant's three questions as our own: "What can I know? What should I do? What may I hope?" Reflections on each of these weave in and out of this book, the first two explicitly, the third never far from view. For many secularists, the decisive question is hope. Although atheism and agnosticism were once energized by confident expectations about where the world was heading, this is no longer so. For this reason, and to soften the vicissitudes of life, many people are tempted to find hope in God. What does a secular outlook offer today? Living without God, are one's hopes fewer, less intense, more realistic, dimmer, or just different?

This essay in twenty-first-century secular philosophy began by exploring the feeling, mood, and idea of gratitude, specifically pointing to forces beyond ourselves upon which we depend and which make us who we are. This dimension, often mistakenly called "transcendent," is usually experienced religiously, but is no less built into our world and our experience. So must I now end by exploring the feeling, mood, and idea of hope, which is also often experienced religiously.

Prior to any religious impulse, and prior to any vision of a world getting better, hope is simply and fundamentally the energy to keep on. Life is hard, often even harder, and sometimes impossible, and we must continuously find within and among ourselves the resources for coping with it: to not give up, to pick ourselves up and start over, to try again, to persist. This energy joins with will, with determination, with courage, with the ability to analyze situations, with exhortations to hang in in the face of loss, failure, defeat, confusion, or tragedy. There is no point arguing over hope, because if it depends on reasons it is probably already lost. Rather, hope springs from the blind and uncomprehending act of keeping on, as the Joad family does in *The Grapes of Wrath*. In fact, it is hope that creates its reasons.

Hope can attach itself to family, or love, or community, or dignity, or principle—or history, or God—but also to nothing at all but the sheer will to not give in. It lives alongside, and constantly overcomes, passivity, despair, and gloom, knowing these intimately but never completely giving in to them. It lives in a fine balance with the negativity all around it and which always threatens to overcome it. There are those idealists who claim to hope but soldier on by denying the negativity, calling themselves "optimists" and always seeing only the positive side of things. And there are those cynics who give way to, and wholly absorb and know nothing but, the negative side. To hope is to steer between these, finding ways to keep on.

Hope is both one of the most deeply rooted personal of impulses and one of the age-old and most powerful social impulses. Marxist philosopher Ernst Bloch tried to connect these in his sprawling *Principle of Hope*, linking all specific and momentary and personal wishes and desires to the greatest of human longings, the expectation that things will turn out all right, finally. Those who believe in God usually project this "finally" beyond the world and our life, but those of us who live without religion want to give it an earthly shape. As do Studs Terkel's interviewees in *Hope Dies Last*.

Although it is not necessarily tied to a specific time, this kind of hope—large, embracing, collective hope—demands that humanity's unending effort to create a decent world will one day pay off. It foresees an end to oppression, exploitation, large-scale conflict, genocide, poverty, and hunger, and an end to the sense of frustration, exhaustion, defeat, and discouragement pervading so many struggles to make the world better. Envisaging, however vaguely, the kind of endpoint that Bloch labels *utopia*, such hope becomes two things Terkel's people live out again and again: the determination to make life better, and the expectation that our efforts will bear fruit. Often when people speak of hope today, they forget the first, the elemental human drive, and dwell on the second, its prospects, the trends and possibilities for its success. They are looking for *reasons* to hope. If they want evidence before rousing themselves, we should ignore them. But once they become mobilized, they are right to look around and assess the prospects. Once engaged, struggling on their own behalf or on behalf of others, they will, should, must get their bearings. At that moment, we cannot avoid asking: Is there reason to hope?

Strolling along Detroit's Riverwalk inclines me to look for an affirmative answer. Nearby are other encouraging projects, including a splendid little city park that offers ice skating in the winter, plans afoot for a striking apartment complex, a new corporate headquarters, and new hotels, lofts, and apartments. A few blocks north are the opera house, the baseball and football stadiums, new townhouses, and a neighborhood being rebuilt that sat vacant for thirty years; and then, another mile up, the stunning Detroit Institute of Arts, just redone. But walk off the beaten path and one encounters decay and silence, a ghost town in places, and scattered and underpopulated neighborhoods in others. This is the Detroit that is one of the most dangerous, the poorest, the most unemployed, and the least educated cities in the country, the once-great Arsenal of Democracy of my childhood that has lost most of its industry and over half of its people in the last fifty years. All attempts at change, and there have been many, seem to run into not only a pervasive sense of how massive is the task and how sparse are the resources, but the knowledge that all the new downtown projects and even neighborhood revitalization must inevitably run aground unless the sickest aspect of the city, its public schools, can become healthy again.

All this can be momentarily forgotten on the Riverwalk while contemplating an older history, captured in the International Memorial to the Underground Railroad. This sculpture and its plaques, along with companions across the river in Canada, celebrate the network that assisted runaway slaves in finding their way to freedom before the Civil War. If alongside Detroit's undeniable downtown improvements lie deeper problems, then alongside these problems lies a memory: Detroit's role in an even more profound story, one of human emancipation. Ascending Hart Plaza at this point eventually takes one to the Michigan Labor Legacy Monument, a graceful and soaring sculpture commemorating the vital role of Detroit's once-mighty labor movement in the city's, state's, and nation's history. And nearby is "The Fist," the monument to Joe Louis, the African American heavyweight boxing champion who thrilled and meant so much to white and black Americans in the 1930s and 1940s.

The Underground Railroad memorial, at the river, sits at a point where I recall standing with my sister and parents, a boy of five, looking across to Canada and hoping that one of my favorite uncles, who was driving an army ambulance in Italy, would come back home from the war. (He did.) Thinking about hope evokes such constant goings-and-comings—between our personal hopes and the ways we share in collective hope, between the will to keep on and the reasons to do so, between what we hope for and all that crushes it, and between our hopes for the future, our struggles in the present, and our memories of the past. Of course much of this goes with being human and we will always live in its back-and-forth. But events and trends in the twentieth century, and so far in the twenty-first, have remarkably changed the ways humans live with their hopes.

First, it no longer makes any sense to expectantly anticipate the advent of the peaceable kingdom, a better world on its way—or even that our children's or grandchildren's lives are likely to be better than ours. One hundred million people were killed in the twentieth century. The Holocaust has happened. So has Stalinism. Marxism is over. Since then there have been Rwanda, Darfur, and Iraq. The basic premises of modernity are in question. We live after Progress, with the exception of a few remaining priests of Progress such as Thomas Friedman, author of such books as *The Lexus and the Olive Tree* and *The World Is Flat*. But humans who live today both without God and without the hopes that supplanted God see ourselves, for the first time in human history, as being truly bereft. Nothing and no one beyond us is protecting us or pointing us in the right direction. Nothing and no one beyond us is guiding the world. No historical logic is making the world better.

After the twentieth century, this cannot help but have a terrifying aspect. The Cold War is over but the bomb is still with us and continues to proliferate. Knowing that humans can use nuclear weapons and can commit genocide, we live without the illusion "Never again." Face it or not, we cannot help dwelling in a permanent sense of danger. Hope without illusion takes us past the piles of bodies, the bombed-out villages, the crematoria, the concentration camps, and the assorted madnesses that created these monuments. When I first formulated this thought, I compared the troubles of those struggling for social justice to those of the Joad family in *The Grapes of Wrath*—their situation worsens each step of the way, and fewer and fewer of them remain to keep on trying. Just when it seems that things cannot get any worse, they do. I confess that the world's story during a large part of my life has felt this way, with the forces of hopeful change weakening every few years. Hopeful movements such as the Prague Spring in 1968, Allende's electoral victory in Chile, the fall of

Portuguese colonialism in Africa, the end of the Vietnam War, the overthrow of the Somoza dictatorship in Nicaragua, and the end of white minority rule in Rhodesia were followed by disaster: the Soviet invasion of Czechoslovakia, the Pinochet coup in Chile, civil war in Angola and Mozambique, the boat people and the Cambodian genocide, the Contra War, and Mugabe's decline into corruption and dictatorship. The first years of the twenty-first century have seen ethnic cleansing, genocide, global warming, terrorism, and war after war.

In the face of such events, keeping on sometimes has become plugging on, without much enthusiasm. But recent years have also seen the end of the Cold War, the collapse of Communism in the Soviet Union and Eastern Europe, the end of Pinochet's brutal regime in Chile, and most remarkably perhaps, the end of apartheid in South Africa. If no one is justified in reflexive optimism anymore, neither does blanket pessimism make sense. Still it seems as if hope has a longer road to hoe today.

The grim side of this story may be among the reasons for a new phenomenon today—the privatization of hope. At its core, hope is both personal *and* collective; one aspect cannot really exist without the other. Beginning in early childhood, individuals learn to hope that good things will happen, that bad things will not—that my parents will come home soon, that I'll get good grades, that my father will take me to the ball game. In our families and at school we learn to hope with others—that our mother's illness will end soon, that our team will win, that the teacher will let us out early. As we grow, we learn both to work to make our hopes come true and to passively and actively share those hopes both in circles of intimacy and with larger groups—that our candidate will win the election, that the winter will be easy, that we will settle the strike, that our petition campaign will convince our congressperson to oppose the war, that we can coax another year out of our old car, that my presentation was convincing, that our plant will be spared the axe, that my medical treatment does the trick, that I'll sleep well tonight. . . . As we become adults, we face one of life's master tasks: finding the wisdom to distinguish when our hopes are personal and when they are social, and to see the links between the two.

My walk along the river testifies to the split personality of hope today. Born less than a mile from here, I drove in from the suburbs to take this walk. My children grew up in the suburbs of "my" city, which is no longer mine because at a decisive moment I felt forced to choose between two kinds of hope, knowing down deep that they could not really be separated. I had concluded that I would not sacrifice safety or decent neighborhood schools for my commitment to my city. Forces well beyond me made it impossible to be whole, and I chose the fragment most important to me. Henceforth I would root for Detroit from the sidelines, work there, spend much time there, but pay nonresident taxes. As far as my city and my family were concerned, the "privatization of hope" was not an abstract formula, but something I lived with a haunting sense of loss.

Today something unnatural is afoot, something new. In saying that hope is becoming privatized, I mean that people are being encouraged as never before to abandon public and social hope, and to seek only their own personal well-being. After the disasters and vast transformations of the twentieth century, children are being raised not only without utopias, but also without a social sense that it is possible to create a better world. They are not being taught to see their private self in tension with their social self, as in my case, but to be unaware of having a social self. They learn to live wholly for themselves and loved ones. No wonder public opinion polls report an enormous discrepancy in the United States between individuals' optimism about their private lives and their gloom about their society.

What distinguishes the newly privatized hope is precisely the mutation that turns public concerns into private ones. We see it in the depopulation of Detroit. One formulates one's hopes in wholly individual terms and then walks—or, rather, drives—away from social problems. Over a million people have abandoned Detroit for the suburbs, and at least that many have left the metropolitan area and Michigan for sunnier places. They have been pursuing their own personal hopes, but hundreds of thousands of individual decisions to give up on Detroit have only worsened the city's problems and diminished the hope of those left behind, while public efforts at renewal, rebuilding, and revitalization have lost steam.

During the past three decades social and ideological trends linked to reenergized conservative movements, especially in North America and Britain, have beckoned us to turn away from the public realm, and the social side of ourselves, as a terrain for improvement and change. We are above all encouraged to organize ourselves around individual responsibility, personal initiative, and private activities. The public realm is slowly being stripped of all but minimal, essential tasks and private enterprise is taking over staffing government offices, operating public recreation facilities, creating and running schools, doing garbage collection, feeding the military, and providing security in Iraq.

The shriveling of collective hope has been powerfully accentuated by the evolution of the most advanced contemporary societies. Not only the global economy but also the Internet and the commercial creativity of consumer capitalism have generated a field of dazzling possibilities for individual initiative. The word "lifestyle" permeates contemporary conversation for good reason. Large numbers of individuals are now free as never before to live as they wish, to travel the world, to sample its diversity, to adopt or design precisely the worldviews, modes of behavior, and identifications they desire. As the American political world has become more contentious and its conflicts seem intractable, and as individuals are free simply to opt out, voter participation trends show that more and more have chosen freedom *from* politics as their personal direction. They see themselves as individuals on their own, asking only to be left alone.

All around us we encounter arguments to withdraw from participating in wider collective hopes, the most eloquently absurd being Margaret Thatcher's assertion that there is no such thing as society, the most recent being George W. Bush's effort to promote an "ownership society" that would bring individual control and responsibility to Medicare, Medicaid, and social security. But the rich possibilities which people see as personal today are really social possibilities. Whether surfing the Internet or walking in the woods, traveling to Bali or falling in love, the truth of our experience, of our belonging—of our being—remains both individual *and* social. To accept seeing ourselves otherwise is to submit to the deadening of a vital dimension of ourselves, a bit like pretending that we do not live in nature, or have no history, or that our ideas make any sense outside of the world that nurtured them. Or, no less absurd, like claiming that our social responsibility and belonging are nothing more than a matter of individual self-interest. We can say these things, and they are being said. But being thus separated from our social side is to be estranged from our very selves. Hope that is about ourselves alone, or confined to our family and loved ones, winds up sounding abstracted, isolated, and unhinged.

The remarkable wave of enthusiasm for Barack Obama that mounted in early 2008, especially among young Americans, shows that this tendency toward the privatization of hope is not irreversible, and that in the world's most individualistic society there remains a widespread hunger for social hope. Hope is one of Obama's main themes: "having the audacity to believe despite all the evidence to the contrary that we could restore a sense of community to a nation torn by conflict; the gall to believe that despite personal setbacks, the loss of a job or an illness in the family or a childhood mired in poverty, we had some control—and therefore responsibility—over our own fate." He clearly understands the connection between hope and action, and his stirring speeches also reflect a keen sense of the difficulty of hope. After all, it entails battling against what Obama calls the "dead zone" of American politics, as well as "struggling with our own doubts, our own fears, our own cynicism." And he is sensitive to the fact that "change will not be easy. Change will take time. There will be setbacks and false starts and sometimes we'll make mistakes."

Obama's inspired words become a chant, and then a song: "Yes, we can." We can change, but change what? What was this former community organizer asking people to do? What are the specifics of his hope? Obama deliberately avoids providing "a manifesto for action, complete with charts and graphs, timetables and ten-point plans." He searches instead for some "of the ways we can ground our politics in the notion of a common good." Although the Obama phenomenon owed much to specifics of the historical moment as well as his personality and identity, he tapped something deeper by stressing the importance of what can only be called moral hope. Obama articulated a vision of community and unity based on acknowledging rather than suppressing differences, and which drew its energy from his capacity, and demand, to feel empathy, to see the world through other people's eyes. The most powerful sentence in his *The Audacity of Hope* stands alone as a paragraph: "No one is exempt from the call to find common ground."

Sounding such themes, Obama has managed to generate a new sense of possibility by reminding a new generation that they are not just separate individuals but social beings. This has been his truly radical accomplishment: to awaken the slumbering social side of millions, especially among the younger generation.

How else might this be revived? Paradoxically, one of the great pathways to becoming aware of our social being is to experience the wilderness. The film *American Values, American Wilderness* reminds us that we are part of something larger, a vast natural world, and have an obligation to it—a collective responsibility toward both our children and subsequent generations. The wilderness makes us aware of ourselves not simply as an *I,* but as *we.*

A third, and perhaps the most important, path for recovering the social side of ourselves lacks the drama of a presidential election campaign or the grandeur of the wilderness, but is available to us in a more daily way. When humans freely plan, cooperate, and voluntarily work together, such activities evoke a sense of fulfilling ourselves individually in a community of mutual respect and self-determination, of giving without demanding in return, of receiving without necessarily having given. These include not only freely chosen collective activities but also a wide range of public and nonprofit organizations we have set up to meet our needs. The first includes co-ops, trade unions, social organizations, activist political organizations, neighborhood groups, and clubs. The second includes such institutions as governments, social service organizations, libraries, schools, colleges, and universities. Despite widespread cynicism and withdrawal, many collective activities for serving and mobilizing our communities nurture a longing for the peaceable kingdom, a societal condition of well-being and harmony.

These activities reflect our social being back to us, and they provide an everyday basis for ideas such as providing for everyone's needs, respecting the rights of all, and ending poverty. Correctly understood, these are not "transcendent" values, but belong to the social lives we are already living. Where do these great principles that many of us take seriously, such as democracy, solidarity, and equality, come from if human beings are not already dependent on each other, if today's wealth was not built on a foundation inherited from the collective past, if every society did not depend every moment on the contributions of its members, if we did not all share basic human capacities to choose freely, to reason, to work, to make moral decisions? Inasmuch as such values are enshrined in the Universal Declaration of Human Rights and International Covenants on Economic, Social and Cultural Rights and Civil and Political Rights, it is not an exaggeration to say that they reflect the hopes of all of humanity, some of history's most marvelous fruits.

Can such visions still inspire people chastened by the disasters of the twentieth century? After Auschwitz, don't we have reason to be cynical about the human capacity and desire to create a better world? After Communism, don't we have reason to be skeptical about massive social change? After Progress, don't we have reason to reject the expectation that technology is making life better? Political actors today must see themselves and their projects with a new humility and sense of contingency. We are still fearful because of the old and deeply inscribed experience of struggling for survival against nature and disease. But whether indirectly, in the shape of nature gone haywire such as global warming or cancer, or directly, most of what frightens us is human. Horror movies and UFOs notwithstanding, until the end of time we are doomed to fear—other people. Sartre described it unforgettably: "Nothing—not even wild beasts or microbes—could be more terrifying for man than a species that is intelligent, carnivorous and cruel, which can understand and outwit human intelligence, and whose aim is precisely the destruction of man." The last century's great lesson is, as Sartre says elsewhere, that "hell is other people." As he became more specific, he had in mind exploitative and oppressive social systems based on domination and inequality and rooted in scarcity. And beyond these, the mushroom cloud is, however grotesque, human power incarnate. Global warming and environmental destruction are a hell that we are making, and cancer and heart disease come less from nature itself than from how we live. And now we also fear crazed men eager to die in order to take with them hundreds and thousands of others.

All of this tells us that humans and the structures we have created, nothing else, are the obstacle to things finally getting better. Whether at Auschwitz or in Rwanda, I would still insist that genocide is not generated out of sin, or because of falling away from the constraints of religion, or out of ineradicable hatreds and drives, or because of technology itself—but from what are ultimately social and political reasons, which can be understood and combated. I would insist that domination, inequality, and oppression, rooted in scarcity—humans against humans—remain the key to what is wrong with our world, and that reversing these conditions remains the key to making it right.

But today hope, as it makes its way, will come to look quite different than the grand hopes of the nineteenth and early twentieth century. Progress from one generation to the next is no longer one of our guiding assumptions. Still, many voices continue to demand that human invention and ingenuity, accumulated in science, technology, and the apparatuses of production and distribution, might be directed at alleviating vulnerability and insecurity. We have already glimpsed some key areas Pippa Norris and Ronald Inglehart point to for measuring this: per capita GNP, prevalence rates of AIDS/HIV, safe water, availability of doctors. The Human Development Index and the annual United Nations Human Development reports tell us with considerable precision how every country is doing, adding key measures of human well-being: life expectancy, literacy, education, and standard of living. To pick only the most important and urgent, the worldwide capacity exists to feed every one of the 850 million malnourished people, and individuals, teams, and organizations keep on working together in large ways and small, planning, organizing, and acting to reach this and the other goals. They insist, in words made famous by the World Social Forum, that "another world is possible."

The most stirring example of collective hope during the last quarter of the twentieth century was the struggle against apartheid, and it has much to teach us. It was an epochal battle against a modern and ruthless power, a subjugated people trying to overcome a systematic form of colonial racial domination. Apartheid set out to organize, constrain, and define the black majority of the population—Africans, Indians, and mixed-race ("Coloreds")—according to the perverted vision and self-interest of whites, above all, Afrikaners. The majority of these, black Africans, were intended to be "hewers of wood and drawers of water" (the exact words of Hendrik Verwoerd, one of the system's architects) for a racially privileged minority. Codified in the Pass Laws, the Group Areas Act, and the strict division of the society into racial groups according to the Population Registration Act, apartheid also entailed hundreds of restrictions in public accommodation symbolized by "Whites Only" signs.

In successive waves of intense activism in the 1950s, 1960s, 1970s, and 1980s, some of the leadership of the African National Congress and other organizations were imprisoned, others were murdered, others escaped into exile, and still others remained on the ground in South Africa. Activists had to constantly overcome passivity and cynicism born from repeated repression. They learned from the twentieth century's revolutions gone awry in a number of ways, including developing an ANC organizational structure that remained coherent and open, drawing upon the full energy of devoted, disciplined, and ideological forces such as the South African Communist Party, while remaining a coalition. They managed to link together a mass movement that set a limited but still-revolutionary goal: minimizing violence, sustaining popular support, successfully rendering the country ungovernable. The leaders were eventually released from prison and returned from exile. They absorbed others from inside the country, and negotiated their way into sharing power as the only force capable of ending chaos and creating a new order.

What resources did people draw on in order to generate hope in the face of the highly organized and crushing force available to the South African state? How did they sustain hope over years of protracted struggle? How do such movements keep on, avoid cynicism, rekindle energy again and again, and above all, retain a belief in themselves and their cause? These are the hope questions. What were the sources of their inspiration, conviction, sense of the rightness of their cause, willingness to sacrifice, and their optimism? A minority of key figures in the anti-apartheid struggle—Desmond Tutu among them—relied on God to nourish their conviction and energy. Communists in the movement began with an equally transcendent sense of participating in the unstoppable force of human social Progress, but by the last years of the anti-apartheid struggle Soviet Communism was dying and had lost its status as a beacon. The vast majority found their hope elsewhere, but where? Without Marx or Jesus, where did it come from?

First, to put it simply, from their own action. By the time of
the Defiance Campaign in 1952, millions of small acts of evasion
had already taken place in buses, bathrooms, stores, and restaurants. Any individual's personal act instantly proceeded from,
demanded, and evoked, solidarity with others. As they created a
counter-community, a mood of struggle, and political structures
of resistance, another world, explicitly *non*racial, became possible.
People absorbed its values, read its writers, saw its plays, listened
to its music. From the beginning, orchestrating demonstrations against oppressive laws entailed planning and organizing
collectively—creating and coordinating groups whose purpose
was to engage in the process of struggle. This in turn placed a
demand on those who had not yet participated: Are you going
to engage in complicity with the apartheid system, or join us and
become active opponents?

Acting illegally against an oppressive system, insisting on defining oneself, regarding those in power as illegitimate, creating
and adapting organizations to fit the circumstances, creating
rituals of solidarity, encouraging a culture of struggle—these
are some of the actions that create hope. It can happen only if
humans at some point draw a line in the sand and resist. Even
when people manage to see clearly into what is oppressing them
and locate appropriate targets, opposition is difficult to sustain:
people become tired, they withdraw, they take the easy way out.
During the most revolutionary periods in South Africa in the
1980s, not everyone joined the movement, and large numbers
of people remained attached to patterns of complicity and
resignation. Hope is frail. Movements may take forever to
achieve their goals, they split and fragment. Left to itself, the
anti-apartheid movement might easily have lost its bearings.

But South Africans looked beyond themselves. They sought
material support for their struggle, and they received it in various

ways from several quarters, including the Soviet Union and Eastern Europe, Cuba, Scandinavia, the countries of the European
Union, and supportive movements in Britain and the United
States. Equally, they also knew, in a way that helped shape their
own identity, that it was unthinkable in a world whose watch-
words had become human rights, democracy, and socialism that
they should have to submit forever to weird, clearly regressive,
and brutal forms of domination. But how did it become unthinkable? What after all *is* this elemental process by which human
social morality had evolved well beyond what the architects of
apartheid were trying to impose? And how *did* South Africans
come to internalize this?

They experienced the hope and clarity that come from seeing
one's cause in other societies' ideals and practices; by witnessing
the independence of black Africa starting with Ghana in 1957;
by hearing about the American civil rights movement winning
major victories against segregation during the 1960s; and by
seeing nearby Mozambique and Angola become liberated from
Portugal in the 1970s and hold on against South African and
American-supported insurgencies. Amid such inspiration and
confirmation old oppressions appear intolerable. One stops arguing theoretically for freedom, justice, and self-determination:
obviously, it is our time, too. By bringing South Africa's apartheid
system before the United Nations, they appealed to the rights
codified in the Universal Declaration of Human Rights, flouted
by their government. All this made majority rule seem right and
inevitable.

In 1955, African, Indian, mixed-race, and white South Africans voiced their aspirations in the Freedom Charter. In its pre-
amble and main points they absorbed into themselves the long
arc of the history, theory, and practice of freedom outside of
South Africa, and added their own contribution:

We, the People of South Africa, declare for all our country and the world to know: that South Africa belongs to all who live in it, black and white, and that no government can justly claim authority unless it is based on the will of all the people; that our people have been robbed of their birthright to land, liberty and peace by a form of government founded on injustice and inequality; that our country will never be prosperous or free until all our people live in brotherhood, enjoying equal rights and opportunities; that only a democratic state, based on the will of all the people, can secure to all their birthright without distinction of colour, race, sex or belief; And therefore, we, the people of South Africa, black and white together—equals, countrymen and brothers—adopt this Freedom Charter; And we pledge ourselves to strive together, sparing neither strength nor courage, until the democratic changes here set out have been won.

Here, as throughout the entire document, we hear echoes of other histories, as well as the new precision given to "all our people": rejecting discrimination by "colour, race, sex or belief." Elsewhere the Freedom Charter promises the end of adult illiteracy, work for all, sharing the wealth of the country, restoring the land to those who farm it, and returning the mineral wealth to the people as a whole.

Today postapartheid South Africa is far less democratic, more unequal, more impoverished, and more insecure than the society envisioned in the Freedom Charter and imagined by many of those who suffered and died for it. Nearly one in four workers is unemployed, the country is riddled with crime and AIDS, most workers continue to commute long hours from the townships, the land and the mineral wealth are still owned overwhelmingly by whites—in other words, in many ways it looks like the old South Africa, despite the spectacular rise of a small black business class and the no less striking appearance of a poor white underclass. Perhaps, then, wresting the state from white control, implementing "One Person, One Vote," doing away with the apartheid system, and creating a new black elite were the limit of possibility. Perhaps other changes can come only long afterward, if ever. Does this mean that the Freedom Charter reached too high? Or was mass illusion about a glorious outcome the only way to build enough steam to make important and major changes happen? And if so, were those who fought against the South African state deluded or cheated?

Unshakable conviction and unrealistic hope probably fed the ferocity required for continuing to demonstrate in the townships in the face of the tear gas, water cannons, and bullets of the South African police. But doesn't everything in this book, including the outcome in South Africa, encourage convictions that are more limited and tentative? Doesn't hope demand that we become rigorously clear about how little can be achieved at any moment? After all, living without God constantly demands this kind of critical self-reflection, the tallying of defeats and dangers, talking honestly and openly about visions of the future being just that, visions.

These would seem to be components of the frail and limited hope available today, and they are not to be sneezed at. But they seem to put us at a disadvantage when encountering those whose determination rests on the transcendent foundation of a supreme being. Secularists experience a problem when facing those whose sense of possibility and rightness are buttressed by a belief in God, or (in the recent past) by an unshakable faith that history is going their way. People may be willing to face death if they think they're serving God, but what about the people who are being realistic, knowing that they are just making some significant improvements in their society? We who are always willing to listen to the other side, who can register so many defeats and betrayals, who can always be wrong. . . . There is nothing to apologize for in this attitude, and if others are more passionate because of their own beliefs, so be it. But it is still worth asking about our strength of conviction: today, what are we secularists, the disillusioned, willing to fight for, to go to jail for, to die for? Or, less dramatically, to live and work for? After the Holocaust, after Marxism, after Progress—after apartheid—what sort of hope animates those who seek social change?

This brings us to the most difficult question of all. Without God, how is it possible to sustain hope over the long haul of a lifetime or the lifespan of a social movement? How can our modest hopes be enough? There are two answers, and they pose ways of thinking about the meaning of human history as well as the meaning of our individual life.

A vital part of the South Africa story, like the story of peace, labor, civil rights, and women's movements, lies in its links with the historical development of human social morality. In the last 250 years, a complex logic has moved from place to place and time to time, from demanding more democratic government, to rejecting the harshest and most brutal forms of oppression such as being others' property, to rejecting permanent and inherited relationships of dominance and subservience—to demanding equality, self-determination, and a decent living. People pick up the baton set down by other people and other movements, at other times, and they go further.

What do we mean when we say that specific forms of oppression, such as slavery, as well as their definitions of human superiority and subservience, have become unacceptable? What do we mean when we call patriarchy a *violation* of human rights? We were not given these rights by God. If we face them fully, without flinching, we will see them as real and historically won norms of human social relations. Colonial rule met a fate similar to that of slavery, as is at this moment happening to patriarchy and homophobia. These have been made, or are being made, unacceptable, immoral, illegal, obsolete. Always a specific result of specific actions by specific people, at any historical moment, human rights reflect a collective and historically expanding determination to be free from domination.

In our own lives we make our molecular contribution to such changes just by teaching our children to accept people of different racial, religious, and ethnic backgrounds, and by living new forms of love relationships. As did our grandparents by going out on strike or fleeing oppression, as did our parents by absorbing and living new ways of treating people as equals and demanding the same treatment for themselves. Sometimes fitful, sometimes sustained, sometimes partial, the determination to be free becomes part of people's identity, occasionally becoming aggressive enough to change habits, laws, and social structures. At times it takes on a moral certitude so powerful that, as in the American South, in South Africa, in countless factories and homes, it gains—always with difficulty because this demands changing people themselves *and* institutions—new workers' rights, gender equality, equal citizenship, and national self-determination.

Such efforts can be crushed, or may run out of steam, or may be, as is the case recently with the results of American peace and labor movements, partially reversed. But, spurred by our modern world's amazing increase of human power expressed in technological capacity, media, productivity, and rising health standards, some among us will not hesitate to push further. As we see with the Human Development Index, people demand placing on the worldwide agenda, against other agendas that are currently riding high such as free-market globalization, the possibility of full development and a truly human life for every last person on earth. Yes, actively hoping that things will turn out all right, finally. Hope is frail, but I think that every time it is experienced collectively, we feel *all* of it. Then we know in our bones that all people are entitled to live free and fully, and well. In the long run this may be as powerful as any belief in God.

Sometimes, then, it is necessary to speak the word "progress." Increasingly humans have struggled for equality and self-determination, and their struggles, and the self-redefinitions they entail, yield concrete results, which may accumulate over time. This is in no way meant as a vision of Progress with a capital P, or to place us in a History with a capital H. I am speaking of contingent and particular human processes. They do not move on their own, or in an upward curve that carries us along—but they only result from people's active, conscious intent, often against powerful opposition, meeting defeat again and again, keeping on despite discouragement and in the face of many negative trends. It is not clear if we will win out, or whether the future holds a deepening of the destructive and chaotic long-term global impasse in which we find ourselves. No matter: the chaos of competing and collaborating trends is unable to obscure the fact that some are more desirable than others, and that in the end it is people, not trends, that will decide the shape of the future.

How does this new sense of history nourish and inspire living and breathing and acting and hopeful individuals? By becoming the meaning of our own lives. This, the second answer, lies within those very times that generate social hope for a better world. Hope lies in those times we act with others on behalf of specific issues of social justice or human rights, or in improving human life—in political campaigns and demonstrations, in out-and-out social conflicts, and less dramatically in patiently and painstakingly working to improve communities in dozens of ways—experiencing such actions as part of a larger human struggle and drawing nourishment and identity from this. These times when we feel hope are no illusion; we actually do experience them. And sometimes this entails being here and now the kind of people we wish to be, momentarily living the morality we wish to realize in the world. Even if only for a flickering instant, we can experience utopia, feel brotherhood and sisterhood toward perfect strangers.

Living in connection with the rest of humanity and the best of its history can open us, even fleetingly, to one of the richest dimensions of existence. Times of collective hope are no less profound, no less worthy of reverence, than what believers in God call *sacred*. What, after all, is the feeling and mood of solidarity? The sense of community? What does it mean to act on behalf of freedom and equality? And what kind of people are we who do this? In sharing these moments, we experience the best about ourselves and others, join this with what is best in the human heritage, and seek to remake the world in its image.

The meaning of life, the meaning of history— living without God, as I have described it, leads us here. But how can I end a book of the twenty-first century by reviving such claims! I know how extravagant they sound in a world of diminished hope. Still, as with any argument concerning important and debatable questions, the truth of what I am saying depends on the agreement of the wider community to which I submit it. We will all find out whether my case is clear, the argument persuasive, the evidence sufficient, and I welcome the debate. In saying that human history without a capital H and our individual lives without God have a shape, a meaning, I am imploring us to not only see and acknowledge this but to take a second decisive step and take responsibility for it, to act to make it so. If this hope and the future it envisions deserves to be kept alive, it is not because *I* say so but because millions of people have moved in its direction over the centuries, bringing it into being and bequeathing us the results. It is from them, and in solidarity with them, that I draw an imperative: to devote ourselves to continuing their work on behalf of freedom and social justice—to make it come true.

Notes

PAGE

Introduction

3. *"looking to a god"*: This is from the mission statement of the Council of Secular Humanism. See www.secularhumanism.org.

3. *in the world*: This is using the figures for atheists and agnostics (4% and 14%) from the Financial Times/Harris Interactive (December, 2006), "Religious Views and Beliefs Vary Greatly by Country," www.harrisinteractive.com/news/allnewsbydate. asp?NewsID=1131.

3. *the Super Bowl*: New York Times, February 7, 2007.

3. *public schools*: Ron Matus and Donna Winchester, "Public: Faith Trumps Science," *St. Petersburg Times*, February 15, 2008, p. 1.

4. *national health insurance*: John Edwards' phrase. See my article, "The New Atheists," *The Nation*, June 25, 2007.

4. *did not exist*: Susan Jacoby tellingly describes the experience of being left out in *Freethinkers: A History of American Secularism* (New York, 2004, p. 3). "It is," she says, "one of the greatest unresolved paradoxes of American history that religion has come to occupy such an important place in the communal psyche and public life of a nation founded on the separation of church and state."

4. *God Is Not Great*: Also published were French philosopher Michel Onfray's *Atheist Manifesto* (New York, 2007), and Jack Huberman's *The Quotable Atheist* (New York, 2006), followed by a flood of other books.

5. *and a minister*: Irving Stone, *Clarence Darrow for the Defense* (Garden City, NY, 1941), pp. 489–91.

5. *greatest one-man attraction*: Kevin Tierney, *Darrow: A Biography* (New York, 1979), p. 399.

5–6. *"Mother Goose"*: This is from a speech given in Toronto (1930), quoted by James A. Haught, *Breaking the Last Taboo* (1996) and on the website www.celebatheists.com/wiki/index.php?title= Clarence_Darrow.

6. *existence of God*: Between 1914 and 1933 the number of doubters and disbelievers rose from 73% to 85% among members of the National Academy of Scientists. As of 1998, 93% disbelieved in or doubted the existence of God. See "Leading Scientists Still reject God," *Nature*, Vol. 394, No. 6691 (1998), p. 313.

6. *with modernization*: According to sociologists who accepted Emil Durkheim's "secularization" thesis. See, for example, David Martin, *A General Theory of Secularization*, (New York, 1979).

6. *the article itself*: "Toward a Hidden God," *Time*, April 8, 1966.

6. *living for today*: For all the lyrics to "Imagine" see www.mersey-world.com/imagine/lyrics/imagine.htm.

7. *flourishing of religion*: Ronald Aronson, "Faith No More?" *Bookforum*, September/October, 2005.

7. *Ronald Reagan*: According to David Domke, speaking of the presidential nominees' convention addresses,

> From 1952, when acceptance addresses began to be televised live, through 1976, Democratic and Republican nominees invoked God on average 2.4 times per address and included common faith terms 11.8 times per address.
>
> In contrast, since 1984 the GOP nominee has invoked God an average of 5.2 times per address—more than doubling the previous level—and included 19.5 faith terms. That's a 65% increase. Among Democrats, Walter Mondale in 1984 and Michael Dukakis in 1988 made only a handful of religious references, but beginning with Bill Clinton in 1992, the party's nominees have averaged 4.3 God invocations and 16.5 faith terms per address—increases of 77% and 40% over pre-1980 levels.

"Religion as a political weapon," USA Today, December 3, 2007, http://blogs.usatoday.com/oped/2007/12/religion-as-a-p.html. See Domke and Kevin Coe, The God Strategy: How Religion Became A Political Weapon in America (New York, 2007).

7. *"public square"*: Obama also defended the separation of church and state and said, to his credit: "Democracy demands that the religiously motivated translate their concerns into universal, rather than religion-specific, values. It requires that their proposals be subject to argument, and amenable to reason. I may be opposed to abortion for religious reasons, but if I seek to pass a law banning the practice, I cannot simply point to the teachings of my church or evoke God's will. I have to explain why abortion violates some principle that is accessible to people of all faiths, including those with no faith at all," http://blogs.suntimes.com/sweet/2006/06/obama_on_faith_and_politics_an.html.

8. *"state is absolute"*: John F. Kennedy, "I Believe in an America Where the Separation of Church and State is Absolute," September 12, 1960, address to the Greater Houston Ministerial Association, www.beliefnet.com/story/40/story_4080_1.html.

8. *"religion of secularism"*: Mitt Romney, December 6, 2007, Human Events.com, www.humanevents.com/article.php?id=23830.

8. *"rather than religion"*: "Bill to Honor Paine Stalls in Arkansas," *New York Times*, February 11, 2007, www.nytimes.com/2007/02/11/us/11paine.html.

8. *"millions of Americans"*: Alan Wolfe, *Transformation of American Religion* (New York, 2003).

8. *do evolution*: Frank Newport, "Third of Americans Say Evidence Has Supported Darwin's Evolution Theory. Almost half of Americans believe God created humans 10,000 years ago," November 19, 2004, the Gallup Organization, www.gallup.com/poll/content/login.aspx?ci=14107.

9. *"in this book"*: The person who posed the question told the panelists that "how you answer this question will tell us everything we need to know about you." Republican Youtube Debate, November 28, 2007, www.youtube.com/watch?v=nClelpvKWTQ&feature=related; for transcript see: "CNN/YouTube Republican Presidential Debate Transcript," www.cnn.com/2007/POLITICS/11/28/debate.transcript.part2/index.html.

9. *Antonin Scalia*: See Jacoby, pp. 348–52.

9. *"schools and government"*: The Pew Research Center for the People & the Press, "Many Americans Uneasy with Mix of Religion

and Politics." August 24, 2006, http://pewforum.org/docs/ ?DocID.

10. *of adult Americans*: It went from 14% who had "no religion" according to the 2001 American Religious Identification Survey (www. gc.cuny.edu/faculty/research_briefs/aris/aris_index.htm) to 16% whose religion was "nothing in particular" according to the Pew Forum's 2008 U.S. Religious Landscape Survey (http://religions. pewforum.org/pdf/report-religious-landscape-study-full. pdf).

10. *"at all important"*: The wording is from the Pew U.S. Religious Landscape Survey.

10. *"prefer not to say"*: *Financial Times*/Harris Interactive (December, 2006), "Religious Views and Beliefs Vary Greatly by Country." www.harrisinteractive.com/news/allnewsbydate.asp?NewsID =1131.

10. *"cosmic force"*: The Baylor Religion Survey (2006) Questions: "The Values and Beliefs of the American Public: A National Study," p. 6, www.baylor.edu/content/services/document.php/33304. pdf.

11. *secularists or humanists*: According to the Baylor survey one in eight of the unchurched "believe, no doubts" and 20% pray daily or from time to time (another 11% pray "only on certain occasions").

11. *shades of disbelief*: While Baylor makes no room available for registering the varieties of disbelief, or of belief combined with disbelief, they do allow ten possibilities for "what do you think God is like?" and sixteen choices of words to describe God. And this important bit of nuance allows them to conclude that Americans believe in four different types of Gods—a significant result.

11. *insufficiently religious*: A stunning example of the "social desirability effect" is the fact that Americans say they attend church up to twice as often as they really do. Such claims are often taken at face value by researchers. See Steve Bruce, *God is Dead: Secularization in the West* (Oxford, 2002), pp. 205-7.

12. *American life*: "Spirituality in America," *Newsweek*, September 29, 2005. *Newsweek*/Beliefnet Poll Results, www.beliefnet.com/ story/173/story_17353_1.html.

12. *24% and 27%*: *Financial Times*/Harris Interactive, "Religious Views and Beliefs Vary Greatly by Country."

12. *six Americans*: Pew Forum, U.S. Religious Landscape Survey, p. 130.

12. *"tacit atheists"*: The expression was used most recently by George Carey, Archbishop of Canterbury. See Victoria Combe, "Britain now 'a society of atheists'," www.telegraph.co.uk/news/main. jhtml?xml=/news/2000/10/28/nathe28.xml.

12. *think about God*: This reference to Jesuit theologian John Courtney Murray's description of the "atheism of distraction," in "Toward a Hidden God: Is God Dead?" *Time*, April 8, 1966.

13. *"world events"*: Baylor, *American Piety in the 21st Century*, p. 30. While it tallies 92% of Americans as believing in God, the more interesting fact is that Pew counts 40% as not believing in a traditional Jewish or Christian personal God. Pew Forum, U.S. Religious Landscape Survey, June 2008 Release, p. 32.

13. *"factual terms"*: "Science, Religion, and the Teaching of Evolution in Public School Science Classes," The National Council of Churches Committee on Public Education and Literacy, March 27, 2006, p. 2.

15. *loss of vision*: Susan Jacoby says that the loss of vision results in a "guarded voice." Jacoby, p. 315.

16. *"hitherto suppressed"*: Alister McGrath, *The Twilight of Atheism: The Rise and Fall of Disbelief in the Modern World* (New York, 2005), p. 178.

16. *"its own values"*: McGrath, p. 219.

17. *illness and disease*: The interest is so intense that almost half of the medical schools in the United States now offer courses on "spirituality and healing." See Claudia Kalb, "Faith and Healing," *Newsweek*, November 10, 2003, www.msnbc.msn.com/id/3339654/.

17. *self-delusion*: Other recent atheist writers are more genial than the two, more willing to debate with believers and discuss issues on the basis of mutual respect. These *"new atheists"* include Julian Baggini, Daniel Harbour, and Erik Weilenberg. See Aronson, "Faith No More?"

18. *"responsible person"*: "The New Atheists"; Leonard Frank, Jean Kemper Hoffman, "Amen to All That," *The Nation*, December 17, 2007.

22. *rituals and life paths*: For me, the outstanding example is the Society for Humanistic Judaism, founded by the late Rabbi Sherwin Wine. See www.shj.org.

23. *optimism peters out*: God survives, but as sociologist Andrew Greeley puts it, "ambiguously, problematically, uncertainly." Greeley,
Religion in Europe at the End of the Second Millennium (Somerset, NJ,
2002), p. 11.

23. *church members*: "Hard Times for the Anglican Church," ZENIT,
November 18, 2000. See www.zenit.org/english/archive/0011/
WA001118.txt.

23. *without God*: Greeley, chapters 3 and 8.

23. *than Americans*: The U.S. figure, 45%, is given in *Newsweek*; the
Canadian figure is 32%. See "Religion in Canada: Its Development and Contemporary Situation," Roger O'Toole, http://are.
as.wvu.edu/o'toole.html. In Canada, as former Premier Kim
Campbell pointed out on Bill Maher's talk show, the people
would be unlikely to elect a candidate for national leadership
who "thought the jury was still out on evolution."

Chapter One

25. *"use its reason"*: Quoted in Jonathan Rée, "The Poverty of Unbelief," *Harper's*, July, 2002, pp. 13–14.

26. *"Age of freethought"*: Jacoby, *Freethinkers*, pp. 151–52.

26. *"king of kings"*: Robert Ingersoll, "Progress," *The Collected Works of
Robert Ingersoll*, (Louiville, 1998), CD-ROM, IV, pp. 475–76.

26. *"his creation"*: Ingersoll, "Ghosts," *Collected Works*, I, p. 217.

27. *"human race"*: p. 201.

27. *"human progress"*: Ingersoll, "The Gods," *Collected Works*, I, p. 97.

29. *"physical world"*: 5.2% agreed. The Gallup Organization (Baylor
survey), "The Values and Beliefs of the American Public—A
National Study," p. 6. The claim is of course absurd as a statement
of atheism.

29. *away from religion*: Bruce, *God Is Dead*, pp. 185-203.

29. *fold as adults*: Cathy Lynn Grossman, "Young Adults Aren't Sticking
with Church," *USA Today*, August 8, 2007, www.usatoday.com/
news/religion/2007-08-06-church-dropouts_N.htm.

30. *"has triumphed"*: Wolfe, *The Transformation of American Religion*, p. 3.

30. *religion itself*: But as it fades, Bruce argues, watered-down religion
is not being replaced by out-and-out atheism, but rather by religious indifference. Bruce, pp. 42, 227.

30. *supreme being: Financial Times*/Harris Interactive. Note that "supreme

being" is not the same as the alternatives offered by Baylor/Gallup, where the first question was: "Do you believe in God or any kind of spiritual force?"

30. *number of secularists*: Bruce describes several different "questionable methods [that] inflate the numbers of the unconventionally religious" (p. 203).

31. *people worldwide*: Phil Zuckerman, "Atheism: Contemporary Rates and Patterns," in Michael Martin, ed., *Cambridge Companion to Atheism* (Cambridge, 2005).

31. *newspaper audience*: See H.L. Mencken, "The Monkey Trial: A Reporter's Account," www.law.umkc.edu/faculty/projects/ftrials/scopes/menk.htm.

31. *"unfit to teach"*: Paul Edwards, "The Bertrand Russell Case" in Bertrand Russell, *Why I Am Not a Christian* (New York, 1956).

32. *"dragon is religion"*: Russell, "Has Religion Made Useful Contributions to Civilization?" *Why I Am Not a Christian*, p. 37.

32. *here and now*: Wolfe, Introduction, and Conclusion.

33. *other countries*: Pippa Norris and Ronald Inglehart, *The Sacred and the Secular* (Cambridge, 2004), p. 215.

33. *religion flourishes*: The best-known proponents of this theory are Rodney Stark and Roger Finke. For a brief formulation of the position and the issues in the debate see Wolfgang Jagodzinski and Andrew Greeley, "Hard Core Atheism and 'Supply Side' Theory," www.agreeley.com/articles/hardcore.html; for their discussion see Norris and Inglehart, pp. 83–110.

33. *"vulnerability is alleviated"*: Norris and Inglehart, p. 5.

33. *insecure world*: p. 231.

34. *equal they are*: p. 217.

34. *"worshiped or prayed"*: p. 220.

34. *more closely*: p. 15.

34. *old age*: "The growth of the welfare state in industrialized nations ensures large sectors of the public against the worst risks of ill health and traumas of old age, penury and destitution, while private insurance schemes, the work of nonprofit charitable foundations, and access to financial resources have transformed security in postindustrial nations, and also reduced the vital role of religion in people's lives." p. 106.

35. *"industrial democracy"*: p. 108.

35. *important to them*: Norris and Inglehart, p. 219. Another powerful historical process is also afoot, leading to a worldwide resurgence of religion. Since childbearing rates are high in poor, agrarian, and industrializing societies and fall sharply in affluent postindustrial societies, the secular portion of the world is in fact shrinking in relation to the religious part. This means that the world is seeing an overall rise in religiosity despite modernization and globalization. Indeed, because of the insecurities and inequalities these generate, growing religiosity might be described as *due to* modernization and globalization. While atheists, agnostics, and secularists might still claim to represent a desirable and possible future, at this moment their relative weight in the world is growing smaller. This is a crucial conclusion of Norris and Inglehart's research. Even in the most advanced societies today, the data chart a trend toward secularization that obviously operates only under very specific conditions and is in no way inevitable. If mass religious disbelief in Europe is a response to material and social progress, for most of the world this is not yet within sight.

35. *security increases*: Norris and Inglehart do point out that even as insecurity and poverty reign in industrial societies, modernization still drives people toward becoming more secularized. And Steve Bruce painstakingly articulates exactly what the secularization thesis is saying and not saying, and then explores the evidence for it, concluding that secularization is irreversible: "The combination of cultural diversity and egalitarianism prevent our children from being raised in a common faith, stop our beliefs being constantly reaffirmed by religious celebrations of the turning of the seasons and the key events of the life cycle, and remove from everyday interaction the 'conversational' reaffirmation of a shared faith" (Bruce, pp. 240–41).

37. *"better future"*: Alister McGrath, "The Incoming Sea of Faith," the *Spectator*, September 18, 2004, www.spectator.co.uk/archives/features/12581/the-incoming-sea-of-faith.thtml.

37. *intellectually bankrupt*: Curiously enough, for McGrath two keys are that atheists are unable to disprove God's existence, and the "atheist case against God has stalled" ("The Incoming Sea of Faith").

37. *"religion of modernity"*: McGrath, *Twilight of Atheism,* p. 221.

37. *"belief system"*: McGrath, "The Incoming Sea of Faith."

37. *"gave it power"*: Ibid.

37. *book-length narrative*: He calls it a "story of the rise and fall of a great empire of the mind." McGrath, *Twilight of Atheism*, p. xii.

37. *grown "old"*: Ronald Aronson, "Finding Faith in Disbelief," *Common Review*, Vol. 4, No. 4, Spring, 2006.

41. *every corner*: Jacoby, p. 132.

Chapter Two

43. *secular culture*: See Dan P. McAdams and Jack J. Bauer, "Gratitude in Modern Life: Its Manifestations and Development," in Robert A. Emmons and Michael E. McCullough, eds., *The Psychology of Gratitude* (Oxford, 2004).

44. *nightfall, for sleep*: And, I must add, since it is an essential part of most orthodoxy, for not being a woman. Solomon Schimmel, "Gratitude in Judaism," in Emmons and McCullough.

45. *within them*: Albert Camus, *The Myth of Sisyphus and Other Essays* (New York, 1956).

45. *"no paymaster"*: Quoted in Frederick C. Crews, "Saving Us from Darwin," *New York Review of Books*, October 18, 2001.

46. *philosophical significance*: For Stephen Jay Gould questions of science should be kept strictly separate from questions of meaning—these are "non-overlapping magisteria." See Gould, *Rocks of Ages* (New York, 1999). But I agree with J. Ronald Munson and Richard Charles York, authors of the *Encyclopedia Britannica* article on the philosophy of biology, that biological (as well as other) sciences set "the limits of reasonable belief about the nature of the living world." "The Philosophy of Biology," www.compilerpress.atfreeweb.com/Anno%20Munson%20EB%20Philosophy%20of%20biology.htm.

47. *"which it preys"*: Charles Darwin, *On the Origin of Species*, Edward O. Wilson, ed., (New York, 2006), p. 498.

47. *"growth and reproduction"*: p. 756.

47. *"favorable transitions"*: p. 754.

48. *"sub-classes, and classes"*: p. 532.

48. *"other animals"*: p. 756.

48. *"in that district"*: p. 498.

48. *"eight orders"*: p. 522.

49. *"deviations of structure"*: p. 510.

49. *periods of time*: As Munson and York put it, "some of the general conclusions of biology have a philosophical interest."

49. *"first breathed"*: Darwin, p. 756.

50. *"giver and receiver"*: M. J. Ryan, *Attitudes of Gratitude: How to Give and Receive Joy Every Day of Your Life* (Boston, 1999), p. 44.

50. *might really be*: In *Rediscovery of Awe* (St. Paul, 2004), Kurt Schneider, although more intellectually serious than Ryan, takes the further step downhill of locating mental health in the region of the mysterious and the unknowable. This is especially odd in a mental health practitioner presenting his ideas to colleagues. Why not begin with the effort to develop real knowledge?

50. *as a whole*: Edward J. Harpham, "Gratitude in the History of Ideas," in Emmons and McCullough.

50. *for the universe*: Daniel Dennett, *Spiegel*, December 26, 2005, quoted in "Media Watch," *Philosophers' Magazine*, Issue 34, 2nd Quarter 2006, p. 9.

50. *"Who Very Much?"*: *Toronto Star*, September 3, 2006. It first appeared in *Philosopher's Magazine*, No. 33, Spring 2006.

51. *natural processes*: Julian Baggini, *Atheism: A Very Short Introduction* (Oxford, 2003), p. III.

51. *"whole life? . . ."*: Friedrich Nietzsche, *Ecce Homo* (New York, 1968), p. 221.

51. *"its blessings"*: Robert C. Solomon, Foreword to Emmons and McCullough, pp. ix–x.

51. *"the universe"*: p. viii.

51. *"most of the time"*: p. ix.

52. *"dependent beings"*: pp. ix–x.

52. *"being on another"*: Darwin, p. 490.

53. *"struggle for life"*: Herbert Spencer, *Principles of Biology: Indirect Equilibrium* (New York, 1896), p. 445.

53. *"Survival of the Fittest"*: See Adrian Desmond and James Moore, *Darwin—Life of a Tormented Evolutionist* (New York, 1994).

54. *meaning and purpose*: High Plains Films, *American Values, American Wilderness* (2005).

55. *"ugly and cruel"*: Gould, p. 181.

55. *"being, evolved"*: Darwin, p. 760.

59. *and on society*: Martha Albertson Fineman, *The Autonomy Myth: A Theory of Dependency* (New York, 2004).

60. *assembled them*: As in relation to nature I might feel vaguely grateful for all the human actions that produce me, but can I possibly feel grateful *to* anyone? If we think about the intentionality of the humans who make us possible, three considerations demand our attention. First, a direct and personal intention to benefit us obviously can be ascribed only to those who actually know us and act toward us: parents, close relatives, teachers, and so on. Second, as Darwin understood, whether those who came before them were fully conscious of this or not, they endured the vicissitudes of life for themselves, but also for their progeny. And further, so that they would survive in their offspring. Finally, although it may appear that we labor solely to provide for our own living, this occurs in social arrangements in which our value comes from our contribution to the well-being of others. Depending on the specifics of those arrangements and the ideology surrounding them, we may experience our participation more, or less, individualistically. But we participate nevertheless, benefiting from and contributing to others. In short, we have clear and specific reasons to feel gratitude to others.

63. *worldly sources*: Examples of the deeply conditioned inability to think of the wilderness without recourse to the supernatural occur repeatedly in *American Values and American Wilderness*.

Chapter Three

66. *"anything is possible"*: Sartre said, in his famous 1945 lecture: "Dostoevsky once wrote, If God did not exist, everything would be permitted, and that, for existentialism, is the starting point" (Jean-Paul Sartre, *Existentialism Is a Humanism*, New York, 1957, p. 5). In fact Dostoevsky did not say quite this in *The Brothers Karamazov*. It is stated in a reflection by Smerdyakov to Ivan on what the latter had taught him: "everything is permitted . . . because if there's no infinite God, then there's no virtue either, and no

need of it at all." Fyodor Dostoevsky, *The Brothers Karamazov* (New York, 2002), p. 632.

66. *Christian Nation*: Sam Harris, *Letter to a Christian Nation* (New York, 2006).

68. *"I was born"*: Hyde is quoted in Robert Fullinwider's excellent "The Case for Reparations," The Institute for Philosophy and Public Policy, University of Maryland, www.puaf.umd.edu/IPPP/Summer00/case_for_reparations.htm.

68. *state-sponsored segregation*: Charles Krauthammer, "Paybacktime," *Prospect*, August 2001, www.prospect-magazine.co.uk/article_details.php?id=3362.

68. *"back of the line"*: Randall Robinson, "America's Debt to Blacks," *The Nation*, March 13, 2000.

72. *Auschwitz and Treblinka?*: The following discussion is drawn from chapter three, "Responsibility and Complicity," Ronald Aronson, *"Stay Out of Politics!" A Philosopher Views South Africa* (Chicago, 1990).

73. *"such plan"*: Charter of the International Military Tribunal, August 8, 1945, in Jay W. Baird, ed., *From Nuremburg to My Lai* (Lexington, MA, 1972), p. 13.

74. *"had happened"*: Jaspers is quoted in Richard A. Falk, Gabriel Kolko, and Robert Jay Lifton, eds., *Crimes of War* (New York, 1971), p. 477.

75. *them, my own*: Jean-Paul Sartre: I am "condemned to be wholly responsible for myself." *Being and Nothingness* (New York, 1956), p. 556.

76. *party leaders*: Raul Hilberg, *The Destruction of the European Jews* (New York, 1979), pp. 703–15.

83. *citoyennisation*: Interviews with the author, July, 2001 and June, 2003. The term is scattered throughout Jeanson's recent writings and interviews. See, for example, Francis Jeanson and Christiane Philip, *Entre-deux* (Bordeaux, 2000); and Francis Jeanson, "Pour une dialectisation du local et du mondial," *Le Passant ordinaire*, Septembre 2001–Octobre 2001.

84. *their community*: Phyllis Aronson, in her role as founding chair of the Huntington Woods (MI) Peace, Citizenship and Education Project, in discussion with the author, July, 2004: www.hwpeace.org.

85. *different but the same*: William Bennett, ed., *The Book of Virtues* (Carmel, NY, 1993); Colin Greer and Herbert Kohl, eds., *A Call to Character* (New York, 1995).

85. *accepted social practice*: This next discussion is drawn from chapter ten, "We Should Be Talking About Right and Wrong," Ronald Aronson, *After Marxism* (New York, 1995).

87. *for all people*: She proclaimed this in her speech submitting it to the United Nations General Assembly, www.udhr.org/history.

87. *"political rights"* Universal Declaration of Human Rights, www.un.org/Overview/rights.html; International Covenant on Civil and Political Rights, www.unhchr.ch/html/menu3/b/a_ccpr.htm; International Covenant on Economic, Social, and Cultural Rights, www.unhchr.ch/html/menu3/b/a_cescr.htm.

Chapter Four

91. *"national origin"*: Approved Ballot Language, www.michigan.gov/documents/Bal_Lang_MCRI_152610_7.pdf.

95. *"anything you want"*: Mira Nair, *The Namesake* (2006).

95. *somewhere in between*: See Pamela Aronson, "Breaking Barriers or Locked Out? Class-Based Perceptions and Experiences of Post-Secondary Education," in Jeylan T. Mortimer, ed., *Social Class and Transitions to Adulthood: New Directions for Child and Adolescent Development* (San Francisco, 2008).

96. *"everything he does"?*: Jean-Paul Sartre, *Existentialism Is a Humanism*, p. 23.

96. *"like a stone"*: Sartre, *The Emotions: Outline of a Theory* (New York, 1948), p. 12.

97. *already commenced*: Benjamin Libet, "Do We Have Free Will?" Robert Kane, ed., *The Oxford Handbook of Free Will* (New York, 2002).

98. *"their control"*: Saul Smilansky, *Free Will and Illusion* (New York, 2000), p. 53.

98. *"dismiss them"*: p. 2.

98. *combat the terrorists*: Edward Rothstein, "Exploring the Flaws in the Notion of the 'Root Causes' of Terror," *New York Times*, November 17, 2001, http://query.nytimes.com/gst/fullpage.html?res=9E00EFD6153BF934A25752C1A9679C8B63

98. *for the terrorists*: Senator Carl Levin, answers to questions posed at Wayne State University, Detroit, March 2002.

99. *professionals today*: Hedrick Smith, "Inside the Terror Network," *Frontline*, January 17, 2002, www.pbs.org/wgbh/pages/frontline/shows/network/etc/script.html. And see Michael Slackman, "Stifled, Egypt's Young Turn to Islamic Fervor," *New York Times*, February 17, 2008, www.nytimes.com/2008/02/17/world/middleeast/17youth.html.

100. *"abused his family"*: "Mitigating Factors in the Case," *New York Times*, May 3, 2006, www.nytimes.com/imagepages/2006/05/03/us/20060504_MOUSSAOUI_GRAPHIC.html.

101. *Action in Michigan*: 70% of them (23% of the voters) voted for Proposition 2, while 64% of all whites voted for it. My math indicates that 56% of non-Born Again/Evangelical whites voted for it. See "Ballot Measures / Michigan Proposition 2 / Exit Poll," http://us.cnn.com/ELECTION/2006//pages/results/states/MI/I/01/epolls.0.html.

102. *once thriving community*: John Ford, *The Grapes of Wrath* (1940). In the novel the story is told impersonally, in one of Steinbeck's "interchapters," and in fuller detail. The onus there is, as throughout the novel compared with the film, more sharply on the capitalist system.

103. *self-sufficiency*: Fineman, *The Autonomy Myth*, chapter one.

104. *better themselves*: Jabari Asim, "Did Cosby Cross the Line?" *The Washington Post*, May 24, 2004, www.washingtonpost.com/wp-dyn/articles/A51273-2004May24.html.

104. *urgent step?*: See Michael Eric Dyson, *Is Bill Cosby Right? Or Has the Black Middle Class Lost Its Mind?* (New York, 2005). See also Dyson's talking points at www.michaelericdyson.com/cosby/points.html.

105. *"human brain"*: Jürgen Habermas, "The Language Game of Responsible Agency and the Problem of Free Will: How Can Epistemic Dualism Be Reconciled with Ontological Monism?" *Philosophical Explorations*, Volume 10, Issue 1 (March 2007).

107. *who they are*: Jerrold Seigel, *The Idea of the Self: Thought and Experience in Western Europe since the Seventeenth Century* (Cambridge, 2005), pp. 5–6.

107. *ability to reflect*: As paleontologist Steven Mithen and philosopher

Daniel Dennett both point out in very different ways, Mithen in *The Prehistory of the Mind* (London, 1996), Dennett in *Freedom Evolves* (New York, 2003).

107. *natural phenomena*: Julian Jaynes, *The Origin of Consciousness in the Breakdown of the Bicameral Mind* (Boston, 1976), pp. 67–83.

110. *in the attacks*: The polls between March and September of 2006, for example, showed that between 29% and 46% of Americans continued to hold this belief, with of course no evidence to confirm it. See for example www.angus-reid.com/polls/index.cfm/fuseaction/viewItem/itemID/13081.

112. *"unlivable situation"*: Jean-Paul Sartre, Forward, R. D. Laing and D. G. Cooper, *Reason and Violence: A Decade of Sartre's Philosophy 1950–1960* (London, 1964), p. 7.

112. *"has given him"*: Jean-Paul Sartre, "An Interview with Sartre," *New York Review of Books*, March 26, 1970, p. 22.

113. *"social world"*: Sartre, *Search for a Method* (New York, 1963), p. 87.

117. *to the deity*: Marcel Gauchet, *The Disenchantment of the World: A Political History of Religion* (Princeton, 1997).

121. *affirmative action*: Exit polls are at www.cnn.com/ELECTION/2006//pages/results/states/MI/I/01/epolls.0.html.

121. *union families*: This is a rough calculation, arrived at by taking the 2006 official Michigan election results total of 3,696,701 votes on Proposition 2 (of which 2,141,010 were in favor and 1,555,691 opposed) and multiplying by the percentage (35%) belonging to union families. The resulting vote for and against can then be adjusted according to the national proportion of black (14.5%) and white (11.7%) union membership in 2006 (according to the Bureau of Labor Statistics "Union Members in 2006," www.bls.gov/news.release/union2.nr0.htm) and the overall black vote for (14%) and against (86%) Proposition 2. While overall 64% of whites voted for and 36% against Proposition 2, this calculation shows approximately 56% of white union members voting for Proposition 2 and 44% voting against. A final step in making the estimate would be to subtract the roughly 35% of union members from the total white vote, which would of course raise the percentage of those remaining who favored Proposition 2 and lower those opposing it.

121. *other whites*: According to the 2004 Pew Survey, evangelicals

favor the public display of the Ten Commandments by an 11 to 1 ratio. See http://pewforum.org/publications/surveys/ten-commandments.pdf. Those self-identifying in the Michigan exit poll as "white evangelical/born again" voted 70% to 30% for Proposition 2.

Chapter Five

123 *refuse to study evolution*: See "Reading the Polls on Evolution and Creationism Pew Research Center Pollwatch," September 28, 2005, http://people-press.org/commentary/display.php3? AnalysisID=118.

123 *choose to be ignorant*: This chapter was written before the appearance of *The Age of American Unreason* (New York, 2008), Susan Jacoby's spirited historical account of America's "intertwined igno-rance, anti-rationalism, and anti-intellectualism" (p. xx). Jacoby explores at length such topics as the roots of anti-intellectualism in U.S. history, the deleterious effect of the media, the dumbing-down of American politics and education, and the recent rise of religious fundamentalism. While she and I are concerned with many of the same issues, Jacoby focuses on the social conditions encouraging hostility to intelligence and reason, while in this chapter I explore the choice to know or to be ignorant under cur-rent conditions. I am pleased to find that several of her analyses are in agreement with themes of this chapter.

123. *among Americans*: Michael Shermer, *Why People Believe Weird Things* (New York, 1997).

124. *logic or evidence*: pp. 24–43.

124. *witches and astrology*: The Harris Poll #119, November 29, 2007, "The Religious and Other Beliefs of Americans," www.harrisin-teractive.com/news/allnewsbydate.asp?NewsID=1131.

124. *dead (21%)*: Gallup News Service, June 16, 2005, "Three in Four Americans Believe in Paranormal," www.gallup.com/poll/16915/ Three-Four-Americans-Believe-Paranormal.aspx.

124. *logical reasoning*: See Shermer's eye-opening discussions. Of course the fundamentalist religions assert themselves defiantly against reason, which is why Shermer devotes himself to ana-lyzing creationism. A good discussion of how religion may be

compatible with rationality is in Julian Baggini, "Who Loses in the Truth Wars?" (www.butterfliesandwheels.com/articleprint. php?num=84). Such beliefs would be what Stephen Jay Gould had in mind by his term "non-overlapping magisteria." See *Rock of Ages.*

126. *"of enlightenment"*: Immanuel Kant, "An Answer to the Question: What is Enlightenment?" www.english.upenn.edu/~mgamer/ Etexts/kant.html.

126. *"getting together"*: John Dewey, "My Pedagogic Creed," *School Journal,* Volume 54 (January 1897), pp. 77–80, http://dewey.pragmatism. org/creed.htm.

127. *in the towel*: Sidney Lumet, *Twelve Angry Men* (1957).

128–9. *free speech*: As one of the prosecutors later admitted, "those trials were . . . a stacked deck" and "the defendants really . . . with the jury and in that atmosphere back in those days . . . in the Cold War . . . never had a chance." To gain the jury's acquiescence to a highly manipulated government case it was sufficient to identify those on trial as Communists, as having been at specific organizational functions, and then to read aloud lengthy passages on violence from the fifty volumes of collected works of Marx and Engels. Ronald Aronson and Judith Montell, *First Amendment on Trial: The Case of the Detroit Six* (2006).

130. *accepts evolution*: Data 360, "Belief in Evolution—% of Population," www.data360.org/dsg.aspx?Data_Set_Group_Id=507.

130-1. *set of beliefs*: The Harris Poll #52, July 6, 2005, "Nearly Two-thirds of U.S. Adults Believe Human Beings Were Created by God."

131. *Pythagorean theorem*: This is in the *Meno.*

133. *college life*: Pamela Aronson, "Breaking Barriers or Locked Out?"

135. *equality, and tolerance*: See Michael Eric Dyson's discussion of the prophetic tradition in his *I May Not Get There With You: The True Martin Luther King, Jr.* (New York, 2000) and C. Eric Lincoln and Lawrence Mamiya, *The Black Church in the African American Experience* (Durham, NC, 1999).

136. *of the world?*: Traditional education in societies' stable traditional knowledge used to form an essential aspect of human life, in all cultures and for nearly all of history. Most of what one needed

to know was passed on directly and experientially, by one's elders and parents, during the long process of growing up. By watching, by practicing, by listening, by memorizing stories, young persons acquired the necessary skills as well as what Dewey called the "social consciousness of the race"—the society's historically developed cultural outlook. Dewey, "My Pedagogic Creed," http://dewey.pragmatism.org/creed.htm.

136. *without God*: These are connected with the "scholarship of integration," "scholarship of teaching," and "scholarship of application" described by Ernest Boyer in *Scholarship Reconsidered: Priorities of the Professoriate* (Princeton, 1991).

136. *and themselves*: They are included in *Greater Expectations: A New Vision for Learning as a Nation Goes to College*, published by the Association of American Colleges and Universities, an impressive clarion call to transform American higher education.

136. *"not proficient"*: *Liberal Education Outcomes: A Preliminary Report on Student Achievement in College* (Washington, DC, 2005), sections 4 and 5.

137. *exposure areas*: The complicated general education program of this minimally selective university seems to be motivated by two worries: that its students, left to themselves, will graduate lacking certain necessary skills (writing, math, critical thinking, computer literacy, and oral communication), and that they will be too narrowly educated.

137. *active learning*: And because the program is built upon three core colleges, it is difficult to offer courses across college boundaries. Ken Waltzer, "General Education Models: Pros & Cons of General Education Strategies," presentation at Council of Colleges of Arts and Sciences, Toronto, Canada, November 9, 2000.

137–8. *accept reincarnation!*: The Harris Poll? #90, December 14, 2005, "The Religious and Other Beliefs of Americans 2005," Interestingly enough, in almost all cases graduate study is less liberal, not more, focused on specific content and ever-narrowing skills rather than expanding people's sense of themselves and the world. If anything, it allows less time for exploring deeper life-questions and takes the individual fewer years to complete. www.harrisinteractive.com/harris_poll/index.asp?PID=618.

139. *give us hope*: Shermer, pp. 275–78.

142. *"caused Katrina?"*: Michael Eric Dyson, *Come Hell or High Water* (New York, 2007), p. 177.

142. *"spared the survivors"*: Dyson, p. 195.

144. *"to be free"*: Ronald Aronson, Introduction, "The Ethics of Truth," Jean-Paul Sartre, *Truth and Existence* (Chicago, 1992); Sartre, p. 52.

146. *"go anywhere"*: Ophelia Benson and Jeremy Stangroom, *Why Truth Matters* (London, 2006), p. 180.

146. *for discussion*: Jürgen Habermas has written a number of works developing this theme, above all *Theory of Communicative Action*, 2 vols. (Boston, 1982, 1987).

146. *religious faith*: Cornelia Dean, "'55 'Origin of Life' Paper is Retracted," *The New York Times*, October 25, 2007, A18.

147. *lack of exercise*: *Affairs of the Heart*, PBS Documentary, #4, "How's Your Heart?"

Chapter Six

151. *beyond this life*: This may also be true of believers in God today, as one of those engaged in such speculation, Hans Küng, reflected before being stripped of his right to teach Catholic theology for such untraditional thinking, "The all-embracing secularization process has produced a shift of consciousness from the hereafter to the here and now, from life after death to life before death, from yearning for heaven to fidelity to earth." Küng, *Eternal Life* (Garden City, NY, 1985), p. 6.

152. *"we are not"*: Epicurus, *Letters, Principal Doctrines, and Vatican Sayings* (Indianapolis, 1964), p. 60; tr. changed.

152. *"for immortality"*: "Letter to Menoeceus," Ibid., p. 54.

153. *"sun-filled days"*: Ernest Becker, *The Denial of Death* (New York, 1974), p. 27.

154. *"demeaning life"*: Robert C. Solomon, "Death Fetishism, Morbid Solipsism?" Jeff Malpas and Robert C. Solomon, *Death and Philosophy* (London, 1998), p. 173.

154. *"is meaningless"*: Thomas Lynch, *The Undertaking: Life Studies from the Dismal Trade* (New York, 1997), p. 117.

154. *"that matters"*: p. 21.

154. *"this difference"*: p. 117.

154. *"out of death"*: Solomon, p. 165.

155. *gratification of religion*: Sigmund Freud, *The Future of an Illusion, Standard Edition of the Works of Sigmund Freud* (London, 1957), vol XXI.

155. *"problem of death"*: Solomon, p. 203.

155. *"death, and reality"*: Ibid.

155. *"vitality and vision"*: Robert Jay Lifton, *The Broken Connection* (New York, 1979), p. 392.

156. *imagine, to feel*: From *Gilgamesh* to Woody Allen, the *Oxford Book of Death* shows how cultures and centuries have treated death and dying. D. J. Enright, *The Oxford Book of Death and Dying* (New York, 1987).

156. *"same falsity..."*: Leo Tolstoy, *The Death of Ivan Ilych*, in Philip Rahv, ed., *The Short Novels of Tolstoy* (New York, 1946), p. 453.

156. *"follow from that"*: Camus, *The Myth of Sisyphus*, p. 1.

157. *"liberates him"*: Jean-Paul Sartre, "Camus' *The Outsider*," *Literary and Philosophical Essays* (New York, 1962), p. 29.

157. *itself there*: Jacques Choron, *Death and Modern Man* (New York, 1964), chapter one.

157. *"happiness of angels"*: Albert Camus, "Nuptuals," *Lyrical and Critical Essays* (New York, 1970), p. 90.

157. *"no salvation"*: p. 103.

157. *"human condition"*: p. 69.

157. *our mortality*: Zygmunt Bauman, *Mortality, Immortality, and Other Life Strategies* (Stanford, 1992), pp. 31–33.

158. *were a spectator*: Sigmund Freud, "Thoughts for the Times on War and Death," *Standard Edition of the Works of Sigmund Freud*, vol XIV (London, 1957), p. 289.

158. *cannot exist*: Bauman, pp. 14-16.

159. *regretted it afterward*: Rachael Myers Lowe, "Most Parents Don't Talk with Dying Child About Death, Many Regret It Later," September 14, 2004: www.cancerpage.com/news/article.asp?id=7494.

159. *"of the dying"*: Norbert Elias, *The Loneliness of the Dying* (Oxford, 1985).

159. *"everyday life"*: Helen Danielson and Kim Bushaw, "Talking to Children about Death," April 1995, North Dakota State University College of Agriculture, Food Services, and Natural Resources, www.ag.ndsu.edu/pubs/yf/famsci/fs441w.htm.

159. *death is common*: Phillipe Ariès, *Western Attitudes toward Death: From the Middle Ages to the Present* (Baltimore, 1975).

160. *in an afterlife*: Choron, especially pp. 73–83.

162. *"painful episodes"*: Friedrich Nietzsche, "Twilight of the Idols," text prepared from the original German and the translations by Walter Kaufmann and R.J. Hollingdale, "What I Owe to the Ancients," www.mv.helsinki.fi/home/tkannist/E-texts/ Nietzsche/GotDamer.html.

163. *family and community*: Michael Roemer, *Dying* (1976).

164. *muscular stiffness*: This list is inspired by Atul Gawande, "The Way We Age Now," *The New Yorker*, April 30, 2007. However, the author seems primarily to have an eye for aging as a time of relentless debility—this appears in how the article is constructed as well as in its conclusions. This chapter is in some respects a rebuttal to his article.

166. *own experience*: Lifton, pp. 173–74.

169. *"la famille"*: See Ronald Aronson, "Sartre's Last Words?" Introduction to Jean-Paul Sartre and Benny Lévy, *Hope Now* (Chicago, 1996); and Simone de Beauvoir, *Adieux: A Farewell to Sartre* (New York, 1985).

169. *"caricatures of themselves"*: Simone de Beauvoir, *The Coming of Age* (New York, 1972), p. 802.

170. *"entire civilization"*: p. 806.

170. *"intellectual work"*: p. 802.

170. *"person's hands"*: p. 801.

170. *"contributions of age,"*: p. 732. This passage is discussed by Debra Bergoffen, "Between Sartre and Beauvoir: Messianic Hope and the Appeal," North American Sartre Society, Mary Washington University, Fredericksburg, VA, April 5, 2008.

172. *"late years"*: John W. Rowe and Robert L. Kahn, *Successful Aging* (New York, 1998), p. 66.

173. *constantly changing?*: There is little in *Successful Aging* to indicate that we are losing strength, slowing down, aging, dying. Yet recent research suggests that people are quite aware of the losses accompanying aging, and would prefer to acknowledge these rather than striving relentlessly to remain positive. Presentation by Heather Dillaway, "What Is 'Successful Aging' in Michigan

Communities?"' Wayne State University Humanities Center, October 31, 2007.

173. *until the end*: I deliberately use what I understand to be a Sartrean conception of aging, which Sartre himself lived, against Beauvoir's own sense of loss. Ironically, although early on in *The Coming of Age*, Beauvoir acknowledges her theoretical debt to Sartre, in fact she not only argues against what he wound up doing, but in a philosophical sense fails to appreciate the ultimate logic of his signature idea of freedom. See "Sartre's Last Words?"

173. *vast literature*: Also see the account of the death of Socrates in Plato, *Crito* and *Phaedo*; David Hume's death in "The Death Of David Hume," Letter from Adam Smith, LL.D., to William Strachan, Esq., www.ourcivilisation.com/smartboard/shop/smitha/humedead.htm.

175. *"been wrong?"*: Tolstoy, p. 466.

175. *"death from you"*: p. 467.

175. *"what then?"*: p. 466.

175. *"grew quiet."*: p. 468.

177. *through the sewers*: Raoul Hilberg, *The Destruction of European Jewry*, pp. 323–27.

177. *tell the story*: Juri Suhl, *They Fought Back: The Story of the Jewish Resistance in Nazi Europe* (New York, 1967).

179. *"surrender and submission"*: Herbert Marcuse, *Eros and Civilization: A Philosophical Inquiry into Freud* (Boston, 1955), p. 236.

179. *"fulfilled life"*: p. 235.

183. *and contributions*: Jacques Derrida, *Learning to Live Finally: The Last Interviews* (Hoboken, NJ, 2007).

183. *"symbolic immortality"*: Lifton, pp. 18–23.

184. *attitudes and prospects*: Pamela Aronson, "Feminists or 'Postfeminists?': Young Women's Attitudes Toward Feminism and Gender Relations," *Gender & Society*, 2003; reprinted in Verta Taylor, Nancy Whittier and Leila J. Rupp, eds., *Feminist Frontiers* (Boston, 2007). See also "The Markers and Meanings of Growing Up: Contemporary Young Women's Transition from Adolescence to Adulthood," *Gender & Society*, 2008.

Chapter Seven

188. *mistakenly called "transcendent"*: See Patrick J. Deneen, "The Politics of Hope and Optimism: Rorty, Havel, and the Democratic Faith of John Dewey," *Social Research*, vol. 66, no. 2.

189. *earthly shape*: It is no accident that *The Principle of Hope*, originally intended as a Marxist synthesis of all human hopeful attitudes and utterances, found its warmest welcome among theologians, specifically Jürgen Moltmann. See my review essay: *The Principle of Hope*, by Ernst Bloch, in *History and Theory*, Vol. 30, No. 2 (May, 1991), pp. 220–32.

189. *Hope Dies Last*: Studs Terkel, *Hope Dies Last* (New York, 2003).

192. *these monuments*: Ronald Aronson, *Dialectics of Disaster: A Preface to Hope* (London, 1984), p. 191.

194. *loved ones*: See Francis Fukuyama, *The End of History and the Last Man* (New York, 1992) and the commentary by Perry Anderson in *A Zone of Engagement* (London, 1992). These are discussed in my "Hope After Hope?" (*Social Research*, Volume 66, No. 2, Summer 1999).

195. *about their society*: See David Whitman, *The Optimism Gap: The I'm OK–They're Not Syndrome and the Myth of American Decline* (New York, 1998).

196. *personal direction*: For voter participation see www.infoplease.com/ipa/A0781453.html.

196. *thing as society*: This is the right-wing counterpart of Bloch's equally mistaken determination to see every last instance of intimate, personal hope as anticipating a better society in the making.

197. *"our own fate"*: Barack Obama, *The Audacity of Hope: Thoughts on Reclaiming the American Dream* (New York, 2006), p. 356.

197. *"make mistakes"*: Barack Obama, "Obama Speech, 'Yes, we can change,'" January 27, 2008, www.cnn.com/2008/POLITICS/01/26/obama.transcript/index.html.

197. *"a common good"*: The Audacity of Hope, p. 9.

197. *"find common ground"*: p. 68.

200. *"destruction of man"*: Jean-Paul Sartre, *Critique of Dialectical Reason* (London, 1991), p. 132.

201. *standard of living*: Generated by the United Nations Development Program, human development goes beyond human rights

and economic growth and seeks to create "an environment in which people can develop their full potential and lead productive, creative lives in accord with their needs and interests." It seeks to build capabilities "to lead long and healthy lives, to be knowledgeable, to have access to the resources needed for a decent standard of living and to be able to participate in the life of the community." The UNDP issues annual reports grading each country according to the Human Development Index. See http://hdr.undp.org/en.

To further refine what we mean by wellbeing, we can also add other features: physical safety and security, employment security, old-age provisioning, civil rights, political participation, and equality for minorities. See Len Doyal and Ian Gough, *A Theory of Human Need* (New York, 1991).

203. *their own action*: See *The Dialectics of Disaster,* chapters five and eight.

205. *"have been won"*: The Freedom Charter, www.anc.org.za/ancdocs/ history/charter.html.

Index